IS YOUR LIFE PEAR-SHAPED OR PURPOSE-SHAPED?

KAYE HOLLINGS

Ark House Press
PO Box 1722, Port Orchard, WA 98366 USA
PO Box 1321, Mona Vale NSW 1660 Australia
PO Box 318 334, West Harbour, Auckland 0661 New Zealand
arkhousepress.com

© 2017 Kaye Hollings

All rights reserved. No part of this publication may be reproduced, stored in a retrieval system or transmitted in any form or by any means electronic, mechanical, photocopying, recording or otherwise without the prior written permission of the publisher.

Bible quotations in this book are taken from the following translations:

The Holy Bible, New International Version,
Copyright © 1973, 1978, 1984, by International Bible Society.
Used by permission of Zondervan Bible Publishers.

THE MESSAGE: New Testament.
Copyright © by Eugene H Peterson, 1993, 1994, 1995.
Used by permission of NavPress Publishing Group.

Apart from family, all work colleagues, hospital and community contact names have been changed to protect privacy.

Cataloguing in Publication Data:
Title: Shaped
ISBN: 978-0-6481016-7-3 (pbk.)
Subjects: Biography, Christian living
Other Authors/Contributors: Hollings, Kaye

Design and layout by initiateagency.com

Shaped is for all those feeling bent by life.
If you want to be re-formed, and are willing to take an amazing journey of self-discovery, you will travel to incredibly enlightening places and be re-fashioned along the way.

Let your hopes, not your hurts, shape your future.
Robert H Schuller

If malice or envy were tangible and had a shape, it would be the shape of a boomerang.
Charley Reese

Acknowledgements

I would like to thank Michaela Kloeckner, formerly from the Gold Coast Potters' Association, Mudgeeraba Campus, for allowing me to observe potters at work. As I wandered around the class asking questions, it gave me a clearer picture of each stage and insights into the importance of being patient to achieve the best finish possible.

I appreciated the group's willingness to discuss what they were doing and to explain the process, giving me a visual lesson that was of great benefit in writing *Shaped*.

Thank you to Alan Galt for taking the time to read the manuscript, write the Foreword, for helpful editorial suggestions and ongoing support over many years for my work with the mentally ill.

Also grateful thanks to my brother Paul and Becky Bee for their comments, critique and encouragement.

Lastly, heart-felt thanks to my husband Cliff who believed my story should be told and constantly coaxed me to continue to write even when my creativity waned.

Foreword

Kaye joined the Sutherland Hospital Chaplaincy team 25 years ago as a breath of fresh air. Coming with the experience of correspondent for the CEO within one of the largest church welfare agencies in the state, and from a conservative church background, she quickly adapted to the Clinical Pastoral Education approach of 'learning from the living human documents', discovering from the patients themselves what they needed in the way of pastoral ministry. After seeing Kaye at work in the weekly pastoral care groups in the psychiatric unit, I was happy to hand them over to her when I moved to another health area.

It is obvious that Kaye has learned a lot about life from the people she has met in her hospital ministry, the people Jesus called 'the least of these my brethren', and in return, her ministry with them has offered something of that generous love that Jesus so prized.

Her third book, an autobiographical prequel to her beautiful stories *Dawn of Hope* and *Kept by Love*, flows smoothly, joining a series of anecdotes from her own life experiences with a wit and humour that makes you want to read more.

Kaye's account of her grandmother's heroic struggle with lifelong mental illness in the days before there was any effective medication or real psychiatric understanding, is an encouragement for all aware

Christians, and her story of her encounter with the 'Divine Potter' is an inspiration for everyone trying to straddle the secular and increasingly marginalised church world. The description of the horrific conditions in the state mental hospitals only 50 years ago should be required reading for all mental health professionals!

A thorough grounding in classical literature, coupled with her relaxed journalistic style, makes Kaye's story resonate at a time when the focus on the insignificant is pushing out what is really important in life.

Rev Alan Galt OAM

Centre Director

Mental Health Clinical Pastoral Education Centre

Sydney

Prologue

The only decoration on the grave was a broken jar, shining in the sun. Without knowing why, I removed the jagged pieces. An instinctive sign of respect perhaps, or not wanting to think of any further pain or sharp reminders surrounding what had been tormented and difficult lives.

It was 1993. Having inquired at the administration office and received a detailed map of Woronora Cemetery in Sutherland, Sydney, I now stood gazing at the 41-year-old grave.

I had just dropped my two daughters at their high school and neither had commented on the low-backed beach chair or coffee and crackers sitting on the back seat. They knew I often spent the day in some scenic spot writing articles so this was simply another ordinary day to them.

Grey granite filled with white marble chips, interspersed with black matted decaying leaves from many yesterdays and more recent wind-blown twigs, gazed back at me. Simply another ordinary day? Why had I come?

The headstone for my grandparents was simple and stark, the lettering faded and weather-worn. Other headstones close by expressed deep feelings such as *Dearly beloved, Forever in our hearts, Always remembered*. This one simply read

SHAPED

In memory of
Ole Johnson
Died 19.11.1952 Aged 72
Irene Johnson
Died 21.8.1970 Aged 74
In God's Care

My grandfather, who had occupied this grave for 18 years before Irene joined him, was just a vague memory to me and hardly remembered. Although he had been loved by both wife and son, it seemed that this family had always had difficulty in expressing their feelings in appropriate ways.

Ole was a Scandinavian seaman who left Norway in his late teens to sail on wool clippers around the world. He was awarded a bravery medal for his actions to save one of these ships that had been blown over in a violent storm. On settling in Australia he worked on boats, on the docks, spent as much time as possible fishing from his own small launch, and never lost his love of the sea. He also enjoyed working with wood.

Although I couldn't recall his face, my passionate love of the ocean, in fact any stretch of water, is perhaps an inherited and valued gift from a man I never knew. I have always felt irresistibly drawn to the sea in a way I can't explain. It isn't enough to observe its many moods and colours but there is a compulsion to leap into it, diving, floating, swimming, immersed in its coolness and power.

But it was Irene I had come to find. Not even *In loving memory of,* I mused. She had lived, she had died, and this grave bearing her name was the proof. The absence of any emotion in these final words was so ironic as memories of my grandmother were filled with intense feelings which, until recently, were as jagged as the broken glass I had just handled. Maybe by the time of Irene's death there were no other sentiments left. Or perhaps this was a reflection of the unwritten family rule–'Don't allow others to see how you feel; keep feelings hidden and private. They are personal and shouldn't be revealed in public or discussed with anyone.'

I sat thoughtfully with hands touching the warm granite. The sun was massaging my back, birds soared innocently in a clean blue sky and a young tree cast gentle shadows over Irene's resting place. The smell of freshly mown grass wafted past as I saw a lawnmower in the distance keeping the cemetery neat and ordered, the antithesis of so many lives interred here. Like so many others in the cemetery, she had been at peace now for a long time. Had the time finally come for the living to find peace as well?

I thought that rather than carved on headstones, *Rest In Peace* should be worn around the necks of those left wounded and in need of healing in the present. The final three words on the headstone, *In God's Care*, were so appropriate for only he really understood her. We are all in God's care, in this life and the next.

Why was I here? Why now when my grandmother had died 23 years ago? *(See photo page D)*

− 1 −

The floor of the potter's workshop is littered with broken and sharp fragments, discarded and unfinished.

Dysfunction – a word carved into the psyche of many when thinking of the past.

Ole and Irene had one son named Robert and their life wasn't easy. Ole worked all day and drank all night. His heavy drinking created financial problems for Irene who constantly struggled to make ends meet. Robert adored his father and times spent together boating at weekends were his happiest childhood memories, especially if they caught fish or blue swimmer crabs for dinner that night. The inviting blue water of Kogarah Bay was right at the end of their street at Sans Souci and beckoned often. Many years later my brother and I would swim there with our cousins, continuing the love of water activities. Robert's favourite meal was seafood, a plate of prawns always more preferable to chocolate or any sweet treat that enticed others.

Mother and son had a very close bond but as an only child and a lonely child, he didn't learn how to relate well to others, always hanging back rather than joining in. At 14, although a bright student, Robert left school and found a job working for a cabinetmaker to help the family income. On a recent trip to Norway, I learnt first-hand that many people there still carve wooden animals and other objects for sale, especially during the long winter months when outside work is very difficult. Perhaps my dad inherited his father's wood-working gene. Dad's interest in current affairs, history, and geography never waned and I can recall many evenings over dinner when we discussed capital cities of the world with the atlas open on the table. It was a game we all loved as Dad asked the questions and my brother and I rushed to get in first with the correct answer. Even as an old man, Robert regretted the opportunities to study that were denied him.

For Irene, Robert became much more than her only son. He was her supporter, her friend, her provider, her life. She couldn't live without him and, whether consciously or unconsciously, decided she never would. This decision was the catalyst that was to bring hardship, heartache and confusion into many lives for years to come. When Robert met and fell in love with Marjorie, things became very complicated. One time I asked Mum who the best man was in their wedding photograph and was stunned at her reply – 'Just some guy at your father's work. He didn't really know him but there was no-one else. He had no friends.' They married in 1945 and a psychological drama began that took fifty years to unravel.

Also in that year, Robert had his left eye removed due to glaucoma, had a glass eye fitted, and had difficulty coping with the big adjustment. Having sacrificed the possibility of further education and now with only one eye, he was also deemed medically unfit to serve his country overseas should there ever be another war. He felt a failure, lacked self-confidence and, because his mother had always made decisions for him, was totally ill-equipped to deal with conflict resolution. He chose flight rather than fight when problems arose in his life.

Ole was very kind to Marjorie and when they were together enjoyed each other's company and conversation a great deal. Irene, not surprisingly, never accepted her daughter-in-law or relinquished her possessiveness. She would not share her son with anyone. They all lived in the same house and tension, jealousy and ill feeling were present from the first day of the marriage.

After I was born, and four years later my brother Paul, the house became far too small for us to survive. This had nothing to do with the size of the building. The main problem was that Irene rejected me, having no desire or need to learn how to relate to a granddaughter but idolised Paul who shared equal place with Robert in her affections. Mum and I became the enemies in her mind, Paul the favourite, leaving Dad trapped and confused in the middle, feeling inadequate and insecure. There was no room to grow.

Robert and Marjorie began building their own simple home a few kilometres away. It was a real labour of love. Money was still tight, work could only be done on weekends and when material was available. During these post-war years many items could not be procured and most people were struggling. There were many nights when, exhausted and aching from pushing wheelbarrow loads of sand around the block for concrete making, Marjorie almost despaired. Would this house ever be finished? Would she ever be free from her interfering, unreasonable mother-in-law? The very thought made every ache, bruise and blister worth it.

Finally the four of us moved in. Only one room was finished, the rest being slowly built up around us as Dad had time. We didn't care. It was ours! During heavy rain the low-lying land flooded and long lengths of wood were placed from front fence to front patio so we could enter the house without getting wet feet. Maybe these times of 'walking the plank' had hereditary significance!

The next few years, although tough financially, were extremely happy and we were contented as a family unit. These were times when we could relax and move in a less stressful atmosphere. Play and laugh without interruption. Come and go as we pleased.

SHAPED

Here Paul and I learnt to ride bikes, climb trees, chase the hens and play with our new dog, a collie called Pal. And there was the hilarious day all our silkworms escaped and had to be retrieved from walls, curtains, benches and floor. When the baker called each day in his horse-drawn cart, I would run to meet him, pat the horse, then eat the middle out of the hot half loaf between the front gate and the kitchen. The delicious smell of freshly baked bread wafting down the street would draw me from any game. Paul befriended an old fisherman who walked past our house each day on his way to the beach. Often Paul would find a fish in the letterbox, a special treat from his new friend. These few short years were full of positive, fun memories that would have to last a long time.

One memorable day Paul and I were playing in the front yard when we saw my grandmother walking agitatedly down our street. How could we possibly know that this visit would change five lives in unbelievable ways?

- 2 -

How do you rebuild crushed dreams lying smashed at your feet?

I saw the familiar figure walking frantically towards our house and followed my grandmother inside. I listened quietly to the disturbing conversation that followed. 'The police are still looking for his body. How could Ole drown? There must be some mistake,' sobbed Irene. But Ole was dead. He had fallen from a pier into Sydney Harbour while unloading cargo from a ship and his body was never found. He lived for the sea and died in the sea.

Irene began putting pressure on Dad to move back to her home as ours was too small for a fifth person. 'I can't live alone. You're my only son. You have to help me. Please come back.' Mum was angry, resentful and broken-hearted at the thought of giving up the home they had only just completed, and her freedom to be the wife and mother she chose to be. She begged Dad not to sell the house or the family's right to a life of their own.

Dad felt guilty and torn between the needs of his wife and his mother. Where did his chief responsibility lie? If only he had a brother or sister who could share the load. If he pleased his wife, his mother wouldn't cope and if he obeyed his mother, he would alienate his wife. The power of his mother proved to be greater.

SHAPED

As we unpacked our belongings at Irene's house, I was scared. For months my parents stepped carefully over the broken pieces of shattered dreams and hopes. Grief and heartache seemed to have also permanently moved in. I knew my parents were miserable, my grandmother was bossy and emotionally unstable, and I hated the old, cold, dark house with very few windows. No sunny rooms here, just a long corridor from front to back that divided the house in two, just as surely as the family was split down the middle.

Irene was queen of the castle, dominating and selfish and only happy when her son or grandson was paying her attention. Hers was a very limited world governed by possessive, destructive love, a love that took and rarely gave. Paul alone saw the happy, soft side of Irene. When they were together, all else was excluded and Irene glowed.

These years held very few happy memories for me. I suppose the baker still called but I can't remember. I presume Paul and I still rode our bikes, but I can't remember. Ole's cranky cocker spaniel Skipper was there but he wasn't our friendly dog and would snap at us if we moved too close. He wasn't Pal and couldn't be ridden around the yard. Why was Pal the one to go? The bad seemed to have swallowed up the good in my mind.

We really looked forward to school holidays when we went to Grandma Parry's home. These were treasured times of going to Taronga Zoo and Manly on the ferry, and going to the movies, very ordinary activities that took on extraordinary significance when experienced in a peaceful atmosphere. There were always lollies and special treats and this woman was like a fairy godmother who could make all things right. She was a gentle, generous lady, who we loved to be with and couldn't wait to visit.

Her house was right next to the railway line at Belmore and running across the tracks was considered adventure to us rather than danger. I thought the sound of the trains rattling past at night were like giant familiar friends watching over me. Every year on Boxing Day all the

Parrys would gather here and this became the highlight of the year for me and Paul. The best part of the day was when all the children took servings of Christmas pudding outside, removed the threepenny coins, threw the rest into the garden and went back for more and more . . .

I hated leaving this grandmother's home with its warm, loving atmosphere. Here there were no explosions lurking just beneath the surface waiting to erupt. Here I would often stand in her wide doorway and sing, pretending to be at a concert with no inhibitions, something I never did at home where we had to remain quiet.

Even though Dad and Mum always treated the two of us very fairly, making sure they never perpetuated Irene's favouritism, Irene's rejection of me, coupled with the emotional powder keg we all lived in, resulted in me being a very nervous and unsure child. I was always striving to please so I would be accepted. Perhaps this had something to do with my disturbed sleep patterns.

Often I would sleepwalk, carrying my hard Globite school case up and down the hall, banging it on either side as I went, disturbing the whole household. I would empty out my grandmother's drawers and somehow manage to get stuck behind the dressing table or some other piece of furniture, would wake, and not knowing where I was in the darkness, yell for help. Could this have been a child's unconscious way of getting even with a difficult adult? It was certainly a picture of inner turmoil trying to escape. I also suffered from unexplained recurring stomach pains for which the doctor could find no cause. I often sat at the bus stop crying, not wanting to go to school, knowing the pains were real but with no understanding that they were probably psychosomatic.

I've never really understood why houses were given names in the past. My grandmother's house was called *Myrtle* with the plaque firmly hanging over the front door. It meant 'token of victory'. Although seeming to rule with an iron fist, Irene was always in a prison of her own making, only ever seeing a token of victory.

One morning was particularly traumatic, the details of the event being as clear today as they were all those years ago for both me, then seven years old, and Paul who was three. Some things are never erased from our memories. Dad had left for work and another violent argument was in progress. Irene cunningly never caused trouble when Dad was home but would constantly pick a fight as soon as he reached the street. Why had Mum bought a new item of clothing for Kaye and not for Paul? Why didn't she do this or that?

This day she was yelling about something equally irrational while Mum tried in vain to calm her and restore reason. We were hiding under the kitchen table when the sugar bowl smashed on the floor near me showering me with the contents. I wasn't hurt, just very frightened. Irene became more and more violent so Mum took me and Paul outside. Irene, who was extremely strong physically, followed and pinned Mum to the fence by the shoulders, shouting hysterically the whole time.

The situation worsened and Mum shouted for me to go for help. There was no phone in the house and by now there was blood all over both women's faces, dripping down onto their clothes. Terrified, and convinced that Mum was going to die, I grabbed Paul's hand and together we ran, barefooted and in pyjamas, to the shop up the street where the owner rang for help. We spent a few hours with a kind neighbour and as Irene was taken away in a straitjacket, we were confused but very relieved that our Mum had survived.

It was only as an adult that I fully understood the extent of the trauma that Mum suffered. The next time the family saw Irene she was in Callan Park Hospital at Rozelle and we were all still in shock. She was moved to Parramatta Hospital and weekly visits over a long period brought added stress to an already stressful time. Initially there was no car and Dad insisted that the whole family go together every Sunday.

Mental health care was still fairly primitive in the 1950s and 1960s. Anti-psychotic drugs were just beginning to be developed, treatment was a long, slow process and patients often stayed in hospital for years before recovering. Sadly others stayed for the term of their natural life as relatives refused to sign release papers and left them there to perish alone. Irene's house had to be sold to pay for her care and we moved many times from one rental property to another.

The picture in my mind is perfectly clear - huge iron gates, dazed faces pressed against barred windows staring at Paul and me outside in the grounds. Normally I loved green grass and flowers but here, from a child's perspective, they were a mockery. Nothing was pleasant. These trips to the hospital were a necessary part of life but always a family secret, Dad insisting that we never spoke about the situation to others.

Sometimes we would take Irene out for a picnic lunch in Parramatta Park if she was granted leave for good behaviour. Years later, driving through that park, I still couldn't see it as a place of fun and relaxation. In my mind it would always be a pretend park. Even while climbing with Paul over the cannons placed there after the war, and rolling down the grassy embankments, there was tension. To the observer, this was a normal family enjoying a day out. I knew, sadly, we would never be that.

A few years later, when Irene was out of hospital, our family tried again to build a separate life for themselves, setting her up in a home unit at Cronulla. We moved into a house in Dolans Bay and finally it seemed as if Mum could relax, with each person's role reverting to normal without unreasonable demands being made and where she could be mistress of her own space. It was not to be.

Again Irene couldn't or wouldn't cope on her own and again she manipulated her way back into our home where she remained until her death. However, the rules had changed and Mum was now in charge but the psychological games and manipulation continued with Irene constantly playing Dad and Mum off against each other. In order to cope, Mum took a full-time job at Sutherland Hospital as a cook where she was accepted and appreciated. This time away from the pressure-cooker atmosphere at home gave Mum a new focus and a more balanced life.

When a holiday was planned, Irene told us she was too sick to be left alone so even managed to interrupt recreational time so badly needed by the rest of us. However, these camping trips were great fun as the small early-model Volkswagen, bursting at the seams with five people and Buster the dog, and towing a caravan, meandered through all the eastern states, and to South Australia. Dad knew that the limited power of the vehicle plus the weight of the caravan could cause problems if we were ever stopped by traffic on an uphill slope. Not to be deterred, he practised backing down hills before we left until, achieving just the right position on the rise, the engine kicked in with just enough oomph to get us to the top. Risky but we always made it.

Our arrival would have been heard long before we were seen, with windows down and an extensive repertoire of family favourites shouted to the treetops. We always sang as we travelled with *McNamara's Band* and the *Road to Gundagai* near the top of our list. Dad loved to get away and tour to new places and when not at home, everyone related much better and for a few weeks, stress was shelved and smiles returned.

Another happy activity was when Dad hired a rowing boat and took Paul and me out on Dolans Bay which was just down the road. They loved to fish but I loved to swim so we reached a compromise. Dad dropped me on a sandbar in the middle of Port Hacking with my towel and the latest book I couldn't put down, and picked me up later in the day when he had his catch. Trailing our hands in the water as we returned, we loved these days soaking up the beautiful, peaceful surroundings that Irene couldn't sabotage. To this day Paul and his wife Melinda still live on Port Hacking with boats and canoes at the ready for fun and relaxation.

Although domineering, insensitive and suspicious, when she was well Irene had a dry sense of humour. Many of her expressions were coarse and earthy, gleaned from Ole's colourful, nautical past. One that always sent us into fits of laughter, even though it made no sense, was when she said something was like 'a festered fart in a pickle jar.' Go figure! She also made great scones, the only positive attribute that stayed with me!

Irene was a tough person who coped with the depression years, poverty and a difficult marriage but in the end she could never be free of herself and her demons. Even when not in hospital, she was caged, restless and scheming. In a whole lifetime she didn't learn that true love gives, not takes, and that her brand of loving was always hurtful.

Although still strong physically, she continued to be mentally unwell, had many trips to hospital and was often depressed and suicidal. Her suicide attempts were always during the day when she was alone with Mum, as usual leaving her to deal with the mess. It seemed that this behaviour was manipulation to gain attention as she never took enough pills to do any real damage but it brought us all running to the Emergency Department.

If Mum complained to Dad about his mother's psychological games, Irene would deny everything and be believed. She lied to make Mum look bad. It's a testimony to Mum's strength of character that after all the years of emotional blackmail she held the family together and stayed sane herself.

Dad handled all this by going straight from work to the hotel every night and not coming home until the anger had settled and everyone was in bed. Even telephone pleas from Mum to come home early and sort out a problem with his mother fell on deaf ears. Whose suffering was worse? Irene always favoured Paul, ignored me, barely tolerated her daughter-in-law and controlled her son. The scenario was one of dysfunction and division with Dad still caught in the middle. We tried to block out the tension during these years and of course could not confide in our friends. Keeping everything bottled up inside became a way of life. It was just what we did.

-3-

The Divine Potter picks up the clay.

So far, my life was without shape and form. It was 1963. I was in my final year of high school, and asking the same questions as teenagers everywhere – Who am I? What is life all about? What career should I choose? But I added a few more! What do you do when you're not good at anything? How can I be successful when I don't believe in myself or have any talents to offer? I represented my school on the swimming, tennis, squash and hockey teams, and always passed my exams, but as this didn't even register on my grandmother's radar, I assumed that again I fell short.

I was busy studying, playing sport or lost in a book, having discovered at an early age that escaping into someone else's world was so much more exciting than my own. My obsession with reading has never waned and includes the musty, dusty classics written by Shakespeare, Charles Dickens, Emily Bronte and George Eliot, to name a few, some of which are with me still, living in a special book cabinet for treasured titles. Denial is a great temporary escape but I was about to learn that you can't stay there forever. My only dream for the future was to one day write a novel.

SHAPED

On walking home from a hockey match one Saturday, a friend gave me a brochure for a holiday camp called Teen Ranch at Cobbitty, west of Sydney. It described a great horse program along with other fun activities and also mentioned that you had to take a Bible. Really? Didn't have one, none in our house, and apart from a few half-hearted, short-lived attempts at Sunday School I knew nothing about God. The constant battle to survive had left no time for spiritual pursuits and I was empty and aimless. How bad could it be, I thought. I love horses, want to go riding so I'll pretend I didn't see that bit about the Bible.

From my first visit, I fell in love with the property, the surrounding countryside, the warm people on staff and even the talks about God began to penetrate my thirsty soul. I heard for the first time that God loved me, had made me and I wasn't a mistake. I wasn't useless and if I trusted him, he would guide me, give me purpose and direction, and be with me all the way. This revelation, despite all Irene's negative programming, made me ecstatic.

I went to youth camp to ride horses and was surprised to meet God. While searching for answers, I hadn't realised that my needs were spiritual. My life was completely turned around and it was such a significant moment. Confusion became purpose. Despair became hope. Unhappiness became joy. Stress turned into peace and a seed of self-esteem at last was planted. Irene's rejection for 17 years caused me to always strive to do better, to achieve more than others, to drive myself to be popular. For the first time, my desire to belong and be accepted was met. I was special to God.

Early one morning I was on a trail ride astride a frisky palomino, the wind in my hair, the peaceful green countryside waking up as hooves cantered by and with my new-found faith bursting out of me. I had found life and it was exhilarating. On the top of a hill with a magic view breakfast was bread and sausages cooked in an old black battered frying pan that lived in the fork of a co-operative gum tree. Best breakfast ever.

As the smoke from the fire swirled around us and the horses grazed nearby, I was excited because I knew I now had a future that God would reveal to me.

I discovered I had a mischievous sense of humour, became an annoying practical joker and couldn't stop laughing. There hadn't been much to laugh at in our home as I was growing up and I had a lot of catching up to do. It was as if God had opened my eyes to all the good and positive things around me that I had never seen before and released the laughter that had been smothered. There was also a renewed appreciation of nature, animals and all created things, along with music. I returned home changed and uplifted, seeing myself differently, and determined not to allow put-downs to touch me any longer. I also subconsciously decided to ignore Irene. For many years she became the invisible woman living in the next room but I had no understanding then of her ongoing impact on my self-esteem. My new motto was to enjoy life to the full and I felt freer than I had ever dreamed possible.

After considering the possibility of training to be a Physical Education teacher, I realised that my great love was writing. I had written many poems and short stories and English was always my best subject. Many times late at night, Paul would rush into my room, interrupting my reading, in a panic because he had an essay due the next day and needed me to write it. I applied for several Journalism cadetships and while waiting for a break, began working as a proof reader and continued to write as a freelancer for various magazines.

Around this time I discovered a magic shop that had a wonderful range of trick gadgets like a large blowfly attached to a teaspoon and an exhilarating powder that, when added to the sugar bowl, produced a result like Mt Vesuvius going off. Placing a dog deposit in the middle of my parent's bed, the day after Mum had purchased a new quilt, didn't generate the humorous response I was anticipating, and the realistic vomit I left on my boss' desk one Monday morning nearly cost me my job.

He came in with a hangover after a big weekend and my surprise definitely wasn't appreciated as he rushed again to the bathroom.

Unbeknown to me, my striving to improve myself and be an achiever was still alive and well. I was working full time, taking typing and shorthand classes as preparation for journalism, attending short story and poetry workshops, having singing and guitar lessons, and doing a dressmaking course. On the weekends I played A-grade hockey and was in a swimming squad. I never once wondered why I was always tired and Paul accepted that I was rarely going to be at home! Voltaire once said *God gave us the gift of life; it is up to us to give ourselves the gift of living well.* I hadn't learnt this yet.

I began to earnestly pray for my brother and parents but it never entered my head to pray for Irene. Paul joined me at Teen Ranch on my next visit and also came face to face with God. Together we attended Caringbah Baptist Church and loved all the youth activities. My relationship with Paul wasn't affected by grandmother's influence as I always knew it wasn't his fault that he was 'the one' and, in turn, he felt powerless to change the situation but never used it to his advantage. When Irene moved back in with us, Dad built an extension outside for Paul and gave her his room. Paul loved the separation this provided and it became his hideaway from family friction – his 'away from granny' flat.

My reading list now included many Christian biographies and I devoured books about C T Studd, British missionary to China, India and Africa who founded Worldwide Evangelisation Crusade; Amy Carmichael who began the Donhnavur Fellowship in South India where she opened an orphanage and wrote books of beautiful poetry that I still read; Jim Elliot who lost his life while trying to bring God to the primitive Auca Indians of Ecuador. This last story, written by Elisabeth Elliot in a book called *Through Gates of Splendour,* told of the death of her husband and his team, their struggles and sacrifices, and mentioned the work of HCJB, The Voice of the Andes, in Quito. This was the first Christian missionary radio station in the world, commencing in 1931 and still operating today as HCJB Global, now also involved in health care and education.

This book grabbed my heart and soul. I finished it on the train travelling home from work and by the time I reached my front door, I was convinced that God had spoken to me, saying that my future was in Ecuador as a writer for radio HCJB. My research showed me that to apply to World Radio Missionary Fellowship in USA, the overseeing organisation, I would need to attend Melbourne Bible Institute (now called Melbourne School of Theology) for two years.

Three things happened to confirm my new plans. Firstly, while in church I still had great difficulty finding my way around the Bible, the sermon being half finished before I found the relevant passage. I wasn't happy about this because, as you now know, I like to be good at everything and I felt stupid. The fact that a girlfriend who had been attending church forever found the place for me didn't solve the problem.

Secondly, although I was a little more confident in myself, this progress didn't extend to speaking in public but when asked to read the Bible in a service, I agreed. How hard could it be? Surely I could do this. It was only a short chapter with none of those unpronounceable ancient names like Beelzebub, Ahithophel or Epaphroditus. Whew – hadn't they heard that Bill and Fred were great names for a son? I wanted to do it but with my knees visibly shaking and my teeth chattering, I doubt anyone understood a word I read! My friend's insightful comment was 'Next time wear flat shoes. That was the first time ever that I thought you'd fall off your stilettos. You could have sprained your ankle.' And the third irrefutable sign was that MBI accepted me.

I had six months to save up for the fees and to inform everyone that Ecuador was getting closer. Of course my church was supportive and even my non-Christian boss gave me a warm send off with lots of embarrassing comments about going off to change the world. My parents, however, thought I was crazy.

I was beginning to understand and greatly appreciate all the suffering endured by my mother and how much I had gained by her example of strength, hard work and perseverance through a really tough life. This is her story too as we were on the same side and needed each other. She had begun attending church, was going to ladies' activities and was really enjoying these new friendships. This helped her to gain a small grasp on what I was doing even though it still didn't make much sense to her. I was so pleased that she would have loving support after I left.

-4-

The clay is moistened and thrown on the wheel where it is slowly and carefully moulded, the potter steadily applying and relaxing pressure to produce the desired result.

Like a piece of unmoulded clay, I was in the potter's hands and my shaping began. At the start of 1968 I was 21 years old and on the train from Central Station in Sydney bound for Melbourne and a new adventure with God. Never having been there and knowing no-one, I had no idea what was ahead. From the first day I loved the lectures, soaking up deep teaching from wonderful godly men such as Rev Graham Miller and Rev George Lazenby like a thirsty sponge. Their insights into Scripture touched me and helped me to grow in God for which I am still grateful today. I even enjoyed learning New Testament Greek!

While I thrived on all this new knowledge, I wilted under the copious rules, which to me seemed unnecessary, and this brought out the rebel in me. The female students lived in a beautiful old house with lovely gardens and lawns that had at one time been the residence of Dame Nellie Melba, the much loved Australian opera singer. Initially these quiet surroundings didn't help me to cope in this unnatural 'holy hothouse'. I was used to being free and independent. How could I relate to ministers' daughters, missionary kids and older Christians who knew so much about the Bible already and were soooo spiritual? I needed an outlet from this pressure-cooker atmosphere.

The flowering weeds I placed in a fellow student's glass containing her dentures were not met with Christian love! When the doorbell rang one weekend, I was in the shower and all of the local girls had gone home. So without thinking, I answered it wearing only a towel. Needless to say this was the height of impropriety and a lecture followed. While scrubbing showers on another day, and laughing with my friend doing the same in the next stall, I tossed a bucket of water over the top of the partition in her direction. Unfortunately she had just stepped out and I baptised the Dean of Women who had appeared out of nowhere to see what was so hilarious. I blamed God for giving me such a warped sense of humour but obviously I still needed to learn how to use it more wisely!

Missing all my regular sport and needing to release some energy, late one night I crept out into the garden (strictly against the rules) and proceeded to run laps. Before too long, the principal and some male students appeared with torches to catch the intruder. Not having time to duck back inside, I climbed a tree and stayed hidden in the foliage until they decided the threat was over. That was a close call!

Remember the spoon and the sugar from the magic shop? Oh yes - there was certainly room for them in my suitcase when I packed for college. However, the former health worker sitting at my table, on stirring her tea and seeing the blowfly attached, was so horrified I thought she might faint and injure herself so I did reluctantly dispose of all such items. Unfortunately, after locking a friend in the broom cupboard in the dining room, the principal walked past and let her out before I could return. Seemed like a fun thing to do. Oops! Physical maturity just happens normally for most of us but emotional maturity takes a lot longer.

I couldn't figure out why I received more kitchen duties than my friends. Imagine huge greasy pots, pans and baking dishes, enough to feed over 300 hungry students, an extremely hot Melbourne summer, no air conditioning or dish washers and one disgruntled, sweaty student. That would be me. It was patiently explained to me that as well as finding my way around the Bible, I needed to learn to obey rules even if I didn't like them and to humbly serve. And that included scrubbing the base of the pots, not just the insides! Oh boy – were they for real? In cross-cultural ministry, where many students were heading after college, there would be countless strange customs and situations that would have to be accepted graciously in order to survive and to be an effective Christian worker. I began to submit and was soon greatly relieved to find myself on gardening duty! Beginning a 3-year journalism diploma by correspondence soon after, kept me out of mischief from then on. I was being fashioned and centred, recognising that a vessel that was unbalanced would never stand up.

Because of my interest in Ecuador, I joined several South American prayer groups because I knew the value of praying. However I was stunned when it was announced that lectures would be cancelled next Wednesday so we could have a Day of Prayer. A day? A *whole* day? How could anyone do that? Over many such days I found out that spending time talking to God was a privilege not a chore.

All students everywhere struggle for money and I found myself with only $50 left in my account. A friend needed a warm coat for the cold Melbourne winter so two of us pooled our resources, placed our gift in the wardrobe as a surprise for her, and prayed that God would also provide for us. The next week I received cheques for $30 and $20 from contacts who had never given to me before. Every time I saw that green coat being worn I was thankful for answered prayer and reminded that God can be trusted with every aspect of our lives.

Jewels
glistening, aglow
he drops to his children
below
not earned but bestowed
from the master's mine of treasures
to uplift and enrich
the souls of men.
                  Undeserved Jewels   KH

Mum faithfully sent me a large homemade fruit cake every term which I shared with all my friends so her parcel was always talked about and enjoyed. At the end of my first year at MBI Mum also met God through her Christian friends at church and my fellow students rejoiced with me. Mum began to deal with the bitterness that had understandably taken root in her life and the healing process for the past commenced. She was a warm person who made friends easily and was refreshed as she mixed with others and joined in outings and meetings. She would always lend a helping hand and spent hours making craft items for fund-raising events. Life was still difficult, with Irene always the elephant in the room, but now she had some healthy happy diversions to look forward to that enabled her to cope better when at home.

Two events in my second year at MBI impacted me greatly. One was the death of a much loved senior lecturer, Rev John Searle, a man whose humble faith and wisdom helped everyone who sat under him. He was a spiritual father to all the students and we all attended his funeral. For me it was my first – sad, confronting but victorious. An often-used quote that he lived every day was *True greatness is measured by the depths to which it can condescend.*

The second shattering event was receiving a letter from World Radio Missionary Fellowship advising that my application for missionary service had been rejected. The reason given was that I needed to gain experience in writing for radio and could reapply in the future. This now makes perfect sense but back then I was totally confused. Had I been wrong in thinking God wanted me in Ecuador? Had God used this desire only to convince me to go to Bible College? Wasn't I learning more about God and studying journalism with the sole aim of serving overseas? Now I was floundering like a fish out of water. I didn't share this with anyone as it was too hard to put into words and sharing anything personal was still foreign to me.

As the year progressed I saw two of my friends accepted for missionary work in Colombia and Bolivia, and although I had absolutely no regrets regarding my studies, I wanted to run away from God. Ironic when I was living in the 'holy hothouse'. Where could I possibly go? My attitude was very immature but I was really hurting as my dream crashed around me. However, in true Johnson family fashion, I pretended nothing had changed and outwardly was a transformed student.

Practical assignments through the year included speaking at ladies' meetings and being part of a musical team that did street evangelism at St Kilda beach on Saturdays. Those earlier guitar lessons came in handy. It was the beginning of speaking in public without being a quivering wreck. Small steps but a good start. At this time I had no way of knowing that this was a skill I would need in the future.

Interstate students like me were assigned to a family in a local church to give us a spiritual home on Sundays. The old white combi van stopped to pick me up outside the gates that first week and Jan and Laurie came into my life. Jan was driving and invited me to jump into the front seat with a wide, welcoming smile. Just as I was about to ask where her husband was, a cheery voice called out hello from the back and turning around I saw that Laurie was a quadriplegic strapped into a wheelchair. They had met when Laurie was a patient and Jan his nurse. She fell in love with his gentle demeanour, soft brown eyes and mischievous outlook on a very tough life.

Sunday lunch in their home became the highlight of my week. They were only a few years older than me and friendship instantly grew. Laurie knew how to laugh at himself and mealtimes were hilarious as food went everywhere and no-one cared. We would count the stains we'd accumulated at the end of each meal to see who had won. He would joke about all his problems and chase me around in his chair if I was teasing him, blocking me into a corner until, doubled over with laughter, I apologised. This amazing couple taught me so much about sacrificial love and humility, and empathy for the disabled began that is still with me today.

As 1970 began, I was again home in Sydney wallowing in my first spiritual black hole. What would I tell all those wonderful Christians at my church who had been praying for my future in Ecuador and supporting me? I was very hard on myself, unrealistically so. Surprisingly no-one asked those difficult questions but I felt like a failure and saw this as another huge rejection. I had taken some courageous steps towards self-esteem but at this point I again felt like the little girl hiding under the table while circumstances beyond her control raged around her.

Selwyn Hughes summed it up so well: *A more complete understanding of how negative emotions arise is gained when we see them as resulting from a failure to reach a goal. When I am prevented from achieving my goal, then problem emotions arise. Feelings of guilt and shame suggest a goal we have set for ourselves is unreachable and, falling short of it, we experience inner devastation. When our goals are frustrated and blocked, life becomes very difficult.* [1] Oh the insights that come with age and experience! Although I thought the potter had tossed this piece of unworkable clay onto the scrap heap, he was in fact holding me firmly, all the while trimming and shaping into a new vessel. My first time in the

---

[1] *Every day with Jesus*, January/February 2016, Frustrated Goals

kiln strengthened me for use but left me unadorned and not yet ready for my ultimate purpose.

For a few months I worked again as a proof reader, continued my journalism studies and wallowed in self-pity, unsure of everything. One day as I was reading my Bible these words leapt out at me – *God is light, pure light. There's not a trace of darkness in him (*1 John 1:5, THE MESSAGE*)*. Finally the sun came out for me. The darkness was in me, not God. I was to trust him for new goals, purpose and direction. This was the beginning of recognition of a deep truth that I've had to draw on many times over the years – when facing difficulties, illness or tragedy we often build a high wall of grief around us that blocks out God's presence. He hasn't left us alone but waits on the other side for us to remove the bricks one at a time so his light can filter through and eventually surround us again. Then we are enthused by his touch and empowered to move forward.

He hadn't abandoned me but was waiting for my soul to catch up with my body so the next phase of his master plan could begin. It happened quickly and took me by surprise – an ad in a Christian magazine for an editorial assistant, my application and acceptance. As I began work at the Church Missionary Society in Sydney, I was overwhelmed to realise that I hadn't mistaken God's guidance - I had just been geographically confused! As I wrote a monthly children's magazine and short stories, edited sermons, lectures and papers for publication, I was fulfilled, challenged creatively and so aware that I could use my skills here in Australia and still have a possible impact further afield. My days were spent immersed in missionary letters and reports, some from South America, and I gained an extensive knowledge of how literature played such an important part in changing lives. Continuing to have a passion for learning, I completed a course in Publication and Typography to give me more expertise for this new role. My thirst for knowledge was alive and well but now undertaken for the right reasons and I was no longer driven by the need to impress or be a better person.

Up to this point, my church experience was only with informal Baptist services so I was on a learning curve when it came to understanding all things Anglican and the formalities that came with it. Since my altercations at MBI in regard to my over-active sense of humour, I had unconsciously decided to keep my wild schemes to myself and to behave at all costs. It was so liberating to find at CMS that even ministers and missionaries knew how to have fun and that we didn't have to suppress our personalities to be acceptable. Oh boy – look out world!

This was confirmed for me one day when Bishop Ken Short, formerly a missionary in Africa with his family, had returned to the office after taking a service in St Andrew's Cathedral across the road. I entered the staff lunchroom to make a cup of coffee. Picture this – one very long table down the centre on which one very long bishop, still in his very long white bishop robes, was lying on his back, arms hanging down, shoes kicked off, trying to cool down. He popped up his head, said 'Don't mind me' and began to hum a song. What a beautiful man and how refreshing to work with such people.

Being real without pretence became my next goal. I regularly took Dad's glass eye to the city to have it polished, and I delighted in producing it during morning tea, to the horror of my work mates. Oh well. I guess not everyone is used to seeing an eye removed and placed on the table near the pepper and salt when it becomes irritated during dinner.

I now knew that writing and helping others was to be the pattern for my life, slowly etched onto the clay over the next few years. A friend asked me to visit a paraplegic girl living in a centre at North Ryde. Tracey was lonely, bored, mentally alert and looking for new friends. During these visits I met many others who were far more disabled and for whom communicating was difficult. One man loved to share his thoughts on the headlines in the daily newspaper so I learnt to be patient in listening rather than give up, walk away and add to his pain, and to look beyond the twisted bodies to the real people inside. I joked with them but on the way home, I cried – for their frustrations, losses and limitations. This was the beginning of my emotional toughening as the pot was trimmed further.

The Sydney City Mission ran a Sunday night Coffee Shop in Newtown, an inner-city suburb, which attracted troubled teenagers and I became part of the team, offering hope along with food and drink. There were brawls most weeks and I wished I'd had time to take self-defence classes. Although it had the reputation of being a dangerous place after dark, I had no fear as I walked alone back to my car because I knew God was with me.

The Mission asked me and a friend to organise a girls' club at Waterloo on Thursday nights, another suburb with loads of social problems. The area contained block after block of high-rise low-income flats where kids were often left home alone, so getting the girls to come was easy. Dusting off my guitar that hadn't been used since Melbourne, they loved learning new songs but often failed to apply the positive meaning as the mix of white and indigenous children constantly created tension. We had agreed to always walk the girls home as some were as young as seven. It seems ironic but we were relieved when a child entered an empty home because the alternative scenario was often a very drunk dad answering the door and trying to proposition us. Again we were protected from any harm or danger.

Towards the end of the year Laurie passed away peacefully in his sleep. Later I learnt that Jan had taken up a nursing job interstate and subsequently remarried. What a testimony they had been of trusting God in all circumstances and what a gift their marriage had been for a few short years!

Irene also died in her sleep, not by her own hands as we had expected because of her many suicide attempts. An immovable image of grandmother for both me and Paul is of a disturbed old lady pacing back and forth in front of the lounge room window, watching every movement of the neighbours while vocally condemning all she saw. From continually sitting in the same lounge chair, and moving one foot in a circular agitated action, common to some who are mentally ill, Irene had worn a large hole right through the carpet. She had almost worn away a marriage as well. At her funeral I really resented being expected to view her in an open coffin. I had no final goodbyes to say and no grief but was so angry that Dad thought this was necessary. On her death, rather than peace being restored to our family, Irene left a mountain of hurts and emotional turmoil that took many years to be resolved. Laurie I would miss, grandma I would not.

-5-

Putting a rug over the worn carpet was easy. Patching up four hurting lives was much harder. Part of Irene's legacy was the beginning of psychiatric problems for Dad.

Dad was a very creative man. He built houses, most of the family's furniture, sheds, toys and a large boat. As a child, Paul tried to emulate him, often ruining his tools and good timber, and as an adult, he still gains great satisfaction from building things. Dad also loved music and singing. He sang in the shower, at work, in the car and while mowing the lawn. He sang loudly and in tune and the neighbours enjoyed his bathroom renditions. They even requested favourites! At work one day he launched unexpectedly into song unaware that a workmate behind him was carrying a large tray containing hundreds of screws. In fright, the man dropped the lot.

He was kind and gentle, had a soft heart and often became quite emotional. Touching books and songs would instantly fill his eyes with tears. His Christmas ritual was to dust off an old record containing two narratives – Why I love Christmas and My New Year's Wish for You. We would grin and bear them because we realised how much they meant to him, even though we knew the words by heart. I also still cry in sad movies or books, part of my inheritance from Dad. However, he never learnt to deal with confrontation, always running away from problems and hoping they would simply disappear. I saw his weaknesses, not his strengths.

Paul and I had both subconsciously decided that if we married, we wanted a calm household, one with no volatile arguments or out-of-control tempers. When I became engaged to John, I thought I had met the right man, but when he broke off our relationship over the phone because it was too hard to tell me in person, I was shattered. This was another rejection that devastated me but I came to see that I could never respect someone so weak, no matter how peace loving.

Later that year, knowing we'd both been hurt by broken romances, a mutual friend introduced me to Cliff. Together we had to learn to risk our hearts again and slowly confusion melted away and love grew in its place. It was deep and wonderful and so definite that not one doubt remained. Cliff was neither like Dad nor John. He was a strong guy who could make decisions, knew where he was going and would support me as we journeyed together.

We were married in April 1973 and as we cruised around Sydney Harbour on the *Captain Cook* for our reception, the beauty of the city lights reflecting on the water mirrored my hopes and dreams for the future. Of course we had to have a water component for the big day! Our wedding party were thwarted when we dropped off all the guests at the Quay but, staying on board, were delivered to a wharf on the other side of the Harbour where we'd earlier left our car. We spoilt their fun but still chuckle about our clever escape. It was so romantic, just the two of us, cheekily waving goodbye to family and friends from the deck and watching the boat make gentle ripples as it took us to the beginning of the rest of our lives.

From the start of our marriage we decided to pray together every morning – for our family and friends, our community, significant events happening in the world and for ourselves. We've done this for over 40 years and we learnt very quickly that you can't pray with someone if you're not on speaking terms. Most of the time this healthy habit enabled us to keep the communication channels open, between each other and between us and God. It is a wonderful way to begin each day.

We began a neighbourhood Bible study group in our home and together ran a youth group for unchurched kids at Taren Point. This only stopped when the hall we were using was sold. It was already very clear to me that most of my service for God would be among those outside the church, those who'd been hurt by life and needed restoration.

Cliff continued running his accountancy practice and after the birth of our two daughters, Natalie and Raelene, I stopped work and really loved being a stay-at-home mum. I began visiting friends, and their friends, in hospital. This happened because, while having an operation myself, I was visited by some distant friends who I hardly knew but was so encouraged that they made the effort. After all my trips to 'those other places', these wards were a pleasure and I loved reaching out to people in need and building friendships.

I also began a mothers' study group and had many articles and short stories published. These were often written in long hand under a shady tree by the Hacking River or at Cronulla beach with the sound of the waves inspiring my creativity. Typing them afterwards was never a chore as time spent with God and nature was stimulating and refreshing. However, our present world of laptops and other faster technologies are brilliant and time-saving inventions. After completing a Script Writing course, I wrote two plays every year for special events at our church and Sunday School (Caringbah Bible Chapel) and was happy and fulfilled. There was now also time for more surfing, tennis and squash as well.

After praying for Dad for 12 years, in 1975 he became a Christian. His new faith was real but he struggled to grow and change was slow but he knew he needed strength outside himself to make sense of life. A year later in his mid-fifties, he was unexpectedly retrenched from his job as a cabinet maker and was totally unprepared for retirement. He found himself with no job, no friends, no interests and family relationships that were very fragile. A complete breakdown soon followed with a diagnosis of agitated endogenous depression, and a cyclical pattern of hospitalisation every two years began – 1976, 1978, 1980. He took all the world's burdens on board and was consumed with worry about things that never happened.

He retreated into himself and the singing and creativity ceased. The only good thing in the renewed rounds of visiting hospitals was that by now the family were familiar with most psychiatric wards in Sydney and knew where to park! Dad was never violent like his mother but severe depression immobilised him and brought further heartache to Mum, who despaired of ever living away from the highs and lows, stress and strain of mental illness in a family member under the same roof.

Paul had married Melinda in 1979 which meant Mum and Dad were alone in a house with anxiety and angst bouncing off the walls. Their faith was the buffer that enabled them to keep going but several times Mum rang asking me to help her drive Dad to hospital as he was refusing to go. The conversation went like this before every admission – 'Please let me stay at home. They don't do anything in hospital. I just sit around and I can do that here. Don't make me go.' What do you call it when your dad/husband is begging you not to do it? Tough love. Very tough love.

My relationship with him was still distant. However, during many visits with Dad, my attitude began to change and a compassion and understanding for him and others with a mental illness slowly grew. Some of the barriers between us began to come down and small healings occurred. Dad would point out other people in the ward who had no visitors and tell me their families had rejected them. 'Would you go and talk to Joe?' he asked me one day. 'He is so lonely'. I was happy to spend time chatting with others and recalled thinking that this was a window into my father's caring nature that I had missed.

Whenever dad was 'up' he would decide to move house and at this point they moved down the south coast to Nowra, a lovely area with green rolling hills and beautiful scenery on the Shoalhaven River. However, no matter how inviting the countryside was on the outside, the inner turmoil remained. Dad would verbalise his irrational fears all day every day until everyone within earshot was nearly at screaming point.

After driving two hours to see him, he would spend the first half of my visit saying – 'You shouldn't have come as you could have had an accident, been caught in a fierce storm or had some mechanical failure. You are driving an old car you know.' Then, during the last half of my visit, he'd become even more agitated. 'Please leave now so you arrive home before dark. Hurry up so you miss the worst of the traffic and watch out for all the idiots on the road.' A 24/7 negative focus disturbs even the calmest person and you contemplate jumping off the nearest bridge. Thank goodness the drive home always calmed me down. Anyone familiar with Seven Mile Beach will understand how therapeutic it is as you drive up the steep incline, over the top of Mt Pleasant, and find yourself gazing down on a curving blue ocean with golden sand that seems to go on forever. This view was the soul cleansing I needed.

Where was God in all this? For Mum, the past was repeating itself and the next hospitalisation was particularly traumatic after five good years. It didn't help when a doctor advised that Dad probably wouldn't recover this time, his current condition was as good as it would get, and he may never be well enough to go home.

However our faith and prayers sustained us and with new medication, Dad returned in a much better emotional place, but his depression continued to restrict him for the rest of his life. He found more patience and acceptance of it as the years went by and when he was well, added some hymns to his repertoire, his favourite being *The Old Rugged Cross* which we played at his funeral.

For me, it was a wake-up call to sort out my relationship. I'd always been Mum's staunch supporter but now God was tapping me on the shoulder and convicting me to forgive Dad. I also learnt that being a Christian doesn't immunise you from becoming mentally ill but God's strength will see you through, no matter how difficult the journey becomes.

My love of nature was rubbing off on my daughters as we watched wriggling worms on the path, our resident blue-tongued lizard trying to hide in the strawberry patch and birds demolishing mulberries. Our black labrador Monty and grey striped kitten Frisky provided hours of entertainment as they vied for supremacy in the Hollings backyard animal war. Cliff's lovingly-nurtured vegetable garden took a battering as dog chased cat through the spinach and tomato plants, knocking many to the ground. He wasn't impressed when I stated that we had enough to feed an army anyway and what was destroyed wouldn't be noticed. How much spinach can two young girls eat?

At seven and four years, they were asking questions like 'Why don't birds wear nappies? Who put the smell in carnations? Does the sun have a bed in the sky? Why do grubs like yucky cabbages?' And so in 1983 *Fortesque and Friends* was published by Pickering and Inglis in England, a book of children's poems in which Fortesque was an unexceptional but friendly worm with an exceptional name. This was another situation when I had to accept a long delay. I submitted my manuscript to 32 publishers in four countries over 2 years but persevered, believing God had guided my writing. Seeing my first book in print was further confirmation that I was where I was supposed to be – combining my natural gift of writing with my spiritual gift of pastoral care.

To wipe the tears of naughtiness
to blow that running nose
to kiss those grubby, chubby cheeks
to scrub the neck just so
to adjust pyjama buttoning
to fix wrongly put-on shoes
to repair those grazed and bleeding knees
to praise even when they lose
to pretend it is a big surprise
to enjoy a tuneless song
to tell that story over again
to admit that you are wrong –
is to love a child.
    Fortesque and Friends, Love is, KH

However, the goal of writing a novel, although still there, was a long way off.

We began attending Gymea Baptist and soon were involved in various ministries. I joined the pastoral care team and led a ladies' Bible study group while Cliff was a deacon, headed up the Social Action Group and helped with Friday Forum, a quarterly meeting for business people with a challenging speaker. He was also on the Board of Christian Mission to the Communist World and Overseas Council and was the honorary treasurer of the Christian Democratic Party. Although these were busy years, in 1989 I began to feel restless and at first I thought the problem was in our marriage. As I prayed, I soon realised that my need was spiritual and not something that Cliff could provide. I asked God to show me how to fill this void and an unexpected phone call soon gave me the answer.

Rev George Capsis of Community Outreach Ministries Inc had established several houses for homeless mentally ill youth in our area and was someone I knew from my school days. Even at high school George took a severely handicapped class mate under his wing and angrily pushed aside anyone who made his friend's life difficult, always the fierce protector of the underdog. He was planning on starting a Crisis Service and asked me if I was interested in attending a 3-month course with the view to then head up a telephone help line. Most attendees caught the vision and signed on. My new wheelchair-bound helper Di assisted me in setting up rosters and there were many nights we shared the late shift together and planned how best to meet all the needs that came to us.

We took our share of desperate suicide calls but mostly the crises were of a practical nature such as needing school shoes for Billy, money to pay the electricity bill, food and clothes. One night the phone was diverted to my home and we were having dinner when it rang. The caller lived in a caravan park, had no car or money and was asking for milk for her baby. I jumped up from the table preparing to leave when Cliff quietly said, 'Please sit down and finish your meal. The baby won't die if you take a few minutes to eat.' After delivering a bag of food along with the milk, I realised that the baby wasn't distressed and my short delay caused no bad consequences. There is a cost in caring and we willingly make sacrifices, but in community work there is a crisis every minute of every day and if the helper's needs are continually unmet, he or she won't be effective long term. Burnt-out carers are of no use to themselves or others. Thanks Cliff for a lesson I needed to learn.

Di and I were often out delivering items to needy families and being my usual helpful self, I was always saying things like 'Would you like me to wheel you through the pedestrian crossing so we make it before the light changes?' 'Can I help you steer around that hole in the footpath?' In frustration, she responded with 'When I need help I'll ask for it but I want to do as much as I can for myself.'

Many years later when out with a very independent friend with multiple sclerosis, also in a wheelchair, I did a much better job as I remembered Di's words and kept my mouth shut. She needed my presence, not my help, to enjoy a normal shopping experience with coffee and fun. This same lady one day wheeled herself, dog in tow, from home to the local shops, but hit a crack in the path and found herself in an embarrassed heap on the grass on the verge of a very busy road unable to move. She was rescued by a concerned motorist and in the retelling, while laughing, said it was better to have a few accidents than to be stuck at home. Caring always blesses the carer and we gain so widely from the stoic, courageous and inspirational lives of those who have lost so much.

I had been writing radio spots for some time, challenging others to consider giving God a place in their lives, and in 1989 these were accepted and aired by 2 CBA (now Hope 103 FM), Living Sound, Radio Rhema and Media Commission (Newcastle). My dream of writing for radio had taken 20 years but with these fledgling steps I was being brought into line with divine design. From 1984 -1999 I continued to have articles published in many magazines – *Decision* (US and Australian editions), *Facts for Faith*, *Christian Women*, *Women's Weekly*, *On Being*, *Teen Talk*, *Challenge* and *Insights*.

–6–

The initial bisque firing removes all water from the piece so that later it can be glazed without returning to mud or breaking. The higher the temperature the more impurities are forced from the clay.

My work at the Crisis Centre had shown me that to be a more effective carer would require more training. In 1991 I commenced a Pastoral Counselling course with the Baptist Counselling Service and this became a year of being emotionally dismembered and then lovingly put back together into a more workable whole. I saw that living with grandma for over 20 years, observing violence, out-of-control emotions and unacceptable behaviour had subconsciously taught me that to be 'normal' I should suppress all emotions and that to be strong, was to be in control. I had turned self-control into an art form.

For the first time I shared my childhood experiences and allowed others a glimpse into my past. The relief was enormous and the tears flowed. Finally it became very clear that to help others we often need to become vulnerable ourselves by sharing some of our struggles and heartaches to show we empathise with their hurts. During a visualisation exercise we were taken on a mind journey to discover how God saw each of us individually in the core of our being. The picture given to me was of a shapely bottle of perfume with the fragrance gently filling the space around it, not invasive or overpowering but welcome and soothing. Although I didn't know then what it would look like, it was clear there was an on-going divine plan for me, one that was achievable and the exact fit. If you haven't found yours, don't stop searching.

As the course was drawing to a close I assumed I would return to pastoral care work at church and was looking forward to using my new-found skills but God had another idea. He seemed to be saying that he wanted me to become a Mental Health Chaplain. Where did that come from? I was stunned.

My response went something like this: 'You can't be serious God. I've already visited more psychiatric wards than most people do in a lifetime. You can't expect me to go back and possibly undo all the good I've just learnt. It's too hard. I'm not strong enough. You're making a big mistake. Please tell me I've misunderstood your direction.'

Guess what? My family didn't object as I was hoping they would; I found and was accepted into the Clinical Pastoral Education – Introduction to Psych Course. Begrudgingly I said 'OK God, you win.' Graciously God replied with the words of Isaiah 45:3 (NIV) – *I will give you the treasures of darkness, riches stored in secret places, so that you may know that I am the Lord, the God of Israel who summons you by name.* Wow! What an amazing promise from an all-powerful God. All my objections fell silent. The next day a distressed neighbour knocked on my door and confided that her mother had just been taken to hospital after a suicide attempt. She knew nothing of my past or of my future plans but I was able to comfort and reassure her. What a confirmation! After that, all doubts flew away and I knew that with God's help, I could move into this next chapter of my life.

From my first week at Rozelle Hospital I had a real peace in the midst of very disturbed people. From being on the outside looking in for over 40 years, I was now on the inside looking out, trying to touch this raw reality and see the world through the eyes of the patients. God reaffirmed that I did care deeply as I began feeling their torment.

I encountered a fenced exercise yard attached to an intensive care ward, a part of the old Callan Park complex, where a screaming, wailing woman was pacing up and down. It was a shock to realise I had been here before and I was shaken by the power of the suppressed memory that confronted me. The child visiting Callan Park to see grandma had been terrified. The adult revisiting so many years later was incredibly sad. Although I thought I had forgiven Irene, I now realised there was still some unresolved hurt buried deep inside that needed to be released and that my time here would bring ongoing healing for me.

Alone with my thoughts, I received permission to wander through a disused building, long closed and boarded up because of the presence of asbestos, but typical of the ward Irene had known. There had been up to 60 in a ward, baths in a row down the centre with no partitions so staff could observe you at all times. You were stripped of privacy, dignity and individuality. In the basement were icy stone cells for holding those whose behaviour couldn't be controlled. All parts of this building were hired out to film crews as many themes could be easily presented here among the graffiti, the cobwebs and the pigeons flying in and out of the smashed windows. For those who had lived there, it probably also seemed like being part of a science fiction horror movie.

Dinner was at 5.00 pm, in bed by 5.30 pm and drugged so staff could go home. Patients were imprisoned, there were no programs or activities and it was a real invitation to be aggressive. All became like the worst person and I now recognised their need to pace and scream, to be seen and heard rather than just disappear into the system. In order to be, perhaps they had to be obnoxious. As I looked at the broken cisterns still in place, I saw broken lives and marvelled that anyone had recovered with this primitive care.

Oh Irene! You had so much time to be confused, to blame Mum for the forced separation from Dad and Paul, for added resentment and bitterness to grow. I could sense her heartache and anguish of not being able to stay with those she loved while made to stay in the institution she hated. She always blamed others. What a tortured life with constant inner turmoil and focus on self. Her world was so small and restricted and she was only free from her illness for short periods of time. Sitting on the edge of a rusty bath in this miserable, empty place smelling of desolation, I began to understand, and my lack of compassion for a very ill grandmother changed to a fierce loyalty for others in the same situation. This was a watershed moment as the potter reshaped my heart and began to reveal some of the treasures of darkness.

I looked out a barred window, felt a cool breeze on my face and took in the lovely gardens and green grassy slopes gently meeting the river, and the paths where the public could walk and cycle. It was a restful relaxing spot for a family picnic. Pleasure craft were sailing blissfully under the Iron Cove Bridge and I could clearly see the busy Birkenhead Point factory outlet shopping precinct on the other side. Those drinking coffee in the waterside cafes and observing the building I was in from afar, were no doubt admiring the picturesque view with the sun shining on the old stones and the whole hospital complex having a quaint, peaceful air.

If they could only hear the echoes of the past, the now muted suffering rebounding off these ancient walls. The first three Sydney psychiatric hospitals - Gladesville, Callan Park (Rozelle) and Parramatta (Cumberland) - were all built in the late nineteenth century on the English model with the same materials and floor plans but with some modifications to suit Australian conditions such as wide verandas and higher ceilings. As roads weren't developed, their beautiful, scenic locations on the shores of the Parramatta River were determined by their accessibility by boat. The yachts and cruisers on the river today had no conception of the boat ride to hell that the early patients experienced. *(See photo insert page A)*

Getting in touch with this depth of despair put me in a heavy, sombre mood as I left the building. I am very glad that treatment today has made great strides forward with interesting programs and chemical strait jackets rather than physical ones. I recalled Dad's hospital care and the world of difference in the approach to mental health where most were helped to lead normal lives and given assistance to cope in the community. He had no idea when visiting his mother here at Rozelle that one day his children would come to visit him in a similar place. That place was Kenmore Hospital in Goulburn, another old, stone institution reminiscent of the Charles Dickens era, built at the turn of the century, where we knew the cycle was continuing. The succession of emotional problems often reoccurs in following generations but Paul and I feel blessed to have been passed over and to have avoided what is still a stultifying social stigma.

As I delved into the history of Rozelle hospital, I became aware of some huge discrepancies between the original aim and my memories of the late 1950s and 1960s. Had I exaggerated the grim, hopeless conditions with a child's active imagination? And where were the enormous pillars and entrance gates that had so terrified me and Paul as young children? It was time to find out.

(See photo insert page A)

Dr Frederick Manning and the colonial architect James Barnet were appalled by the overcrowding at Tarban Creek Asylum at Gladesville, the oldest psychiatric hospital in New South Wales, and were instrumental in approaching the government to acquire land on which to build another asylum for Sydney. In 1875 Manning went on leave to England to study the then modern-day asylums and his report produced revolutionary changes in mental health care in New South Wales. On 1 July 1876 Manning was appointed by the Colonial Government as the Inspector General of the Insane. He was noted for his humanitarianism and his constant desire was to ensure that his patients received treatment for their illnesses rather than confinement in a 'cemetery for diseased intellects'.

The building of Callan Park began on 23 April 1880 and was completed by January 1885. Local citizens protested about the feared impact of a lunatic asylum in the area but their concerns were rejected by the government. The buildings became known as the Kirkbride Block, named after the eminent American Dr William Kirkbride, who was renowned for his pioneering work and thoughts on progressive mental health care. Kirkbride's concepts provided for a self-contained community with a variety of wards designed to provide separate accommodation and activities to match the various stages of a patient's illness and convalescence.

The Kirkbride Block was mainly built from sandstone that was quarried on site with two large underground water tanks that each held approximately 1 million gallons of water. The water tower standing 100 feet high was built in Italianate style while the rest of the buildings were Victorian free-classical style. This remains one of the grandest pieces of architecture in Australia. The whole complex gave patients a pained panoramic view of Sydney and the Blue Mountains, and the sloping banks at the rear of each ward, incorporating ha-ha walls, gave the feeling of not being incarcerated.

Ha-ha walls were a feature in English gardens to keep livestock in the park away from the house and were mentioned by Jane Austen in *Mansfield Park*. These sunken retaining walls formed a hidden boundary, an almost invisible ditch not noticeable from a distance. Coming across one is a surprise. In the Callan Park setting, I can visualise a distressed patient trying to escape down to the river and the wall mockingly saying 'Ha ha. Gotcha! You can't go past here.'

(See photo page)

A large pleasure garden for the patients was created and the surrounding 11 acres were planted with native trees and shrubs and landscaped by Charles Moore, curator of the Botanic Gardens in the 1800s. Both Manning and Kirkbride believed that beautiful surroundings would promote healing and Dr Sydney Jones, Medical Superintendent from 1925 to 1948, said that the grounds should be used as 'machinery whereby a patient's mind could be directed from neurosis to normality.' So progressive mental health care was practised and the aims of the hospital were fulfilled.

However, over the next decade conditions drastically declined. The facility originally housed around 650 patients but by 1961 there were 1750 in residence. This gross overcrowding led to violence and oppression and patients often stayed for the rest of their lives. On our visits to Irene, she would beg Dad not to leave her there forever like others she had befriended whose families had both rejected and forgotten them. The emergence of these horror stories led to the 1961 Royal Commission.

Royal Commission of Inquiry in respect of certain matters relating to Callan Park Mental Hospital

Start date: 15 December 1960
End date: 28 July 1961

The terms of reference for the commission were to investigate:
(1) Whether any patients at Callan Park Mental Hospital have been subjected to neglect or cruelty by any member of staff of the said hospital and, if so, in what circumstances, and by whom

(2) Whether money, food, comforts or other articles provided or intended for the use of patients of the said hospital have been misappropriated or diverted by members of the said hospital.

(3) Whether the procedures and methods which have been directed to be observed at the said hospital in relation to the supply and handling of food and other articles for the sustenance and comfort of the patients of the said hospital are being adhered to, and whether any other procedures and methods are necessary to safeguard the interests of patients

(4) The suitability of clothing supplied to patients at the said hospital

(5) The condition, including cleanliness of the accommodation provided for patients at the said hospital

(6) The quality and dietetic value of the food served to patients at the said hospital and the competency of the staff engaged in the preparation of such food

(7) Whether any member or members of the staff of the said hospital have improperly brought into or retained or consumed alcoholic liquor in the premises of the said hospital

(8) Whether there has been –
    (a) any neglect of duty by any member or members of the staff of the said hospital
        (i) in improperly absenting themselves from their place of duty during hours in which they were rostered on duty; or
        (ii) in relation to any deceased patients: or
    (b) any improper conduct in attending to the body of any deceased patient

The Honourable John Henry McClemens was appointed Commissioner.

The Commission held 69 hearings. The Commission commenced hearings on 15 December 1960, and concluded on 28 July 1961.

Findings:

The Commission found that there were some instances of cruelty to patients, and some staff had been disciplined and dismissed for assaults on patients. However the Commission also found that most of the staff were dedicated and caring. The Commission concluded that only a small number of male staff and none of the female staff were guilty of cruelty.

The Commission found that there was no evidence of improper conduct in attending to the body of deceased patients at the Hospital. However, there had been some evidence of neglect of patients which included sleeping on, and absences from, duty by staff particularly in the male wards. The Commission noted that there had been some instances when the cleanliness of patients had been inadequate. The instances of injuries to patients were also found to be excessive.

The Commission found that theft of food was rife in the organisation. One nurse had been arrested for stealing a large quantity of food. The Commission found that there was some evidence of drunkenness of staff on duty, and two members of staff had been dismissed for this.

The Commission found that clothing of male patients was generally unsuitable. The patients needed to have more variety in their clothing, and be able to wear their own clothing. The commission found that overcrowding often resulted in theft of personal effects and clothing. The standard of clothing of female patients was found to be better, but more consultation was recommended particularly with the female staff regarding the design of clothing to fit with standards in the community.

The Commission found that state of accommodation was generally inadequate particularly in the older parts of the hospital such as the Kirkbride wards. However, the atmosphere in the newer parts of the hospital such as the Cerebral Surgery and Research Unit was found to be pleasant and home like. The Commission found that conditions in the male wards were depressing and overcrowded to the extent that, some

> patients were sleeping on the floor. The conditions in the female wards were found to be marginally better. The Commission concluded that overcrowding often resulted in inadequate treatment and classification of patients. The Commission also found that inadequate bathroom facilities resulted in diminished dignity for all patients. The Commission recommended several improvements to the hospital including a new pharmacy, an adequate library, and a dining room.
>
> **The Commission recommended the following reforms to Callan Park**: Improve accommodation, reduce overcrowding, and renovate or rebuild parts of the hospital. The Commission also recommended that a shift in the emphasis of therapy take place, in order to facilitate the rehabilitation, and discharge of suitable patients. **The Commission ended on 28 August 1961.**
>
> *Source:* www.records.nsw.gov.au/agency/4960

As well as learning about the past, every person I met taught me something new. One day I met Jana. She threw herself into the armchair, drew her knees up tightly, put her head in her hands and sobbed. And sobbed and sobbed. People constantly walked past but seemed like shadows. She knew they were there but they were outside her agony. Her world was falling apart and she was torn between helplessness and guilt. Helpless because others were controlling her life and guilty because she was separated from her 18 month old son yet again. It was bizarre and cruel.

Looking up through the tears, she focused on the people who were with her in the ward and became aware that the shadows were real. She wasn't alone and while she was struggling with her torments, they were trying to deal with similar pain and make sense of the paradox of mental illness. They all hated falling into a deep depression after being happy and well; coping wonderfully with motherhood then one dark day leaving the baby on the train; holding down a job and loving it, then being so confused and stressed by changes at work that resignation followed. Like being in prison, they are locked in with themselves and their demons and locked out of the world that they so fiercely want to enjoy.

'Will I sleep or toss restlessly tonight? Will my medication be increased or decreased? Is this going to be a good week or another time of anxiety I inflict on my family? Will I be at peace with myself or will my mind be at war? Will I be collected by the police or the mental health crisis team? Will I ever feel normal?' These dilemmas return in an on-going cycle to haunt and exhaust.

Jana imagined a graph of her life. As well as a line ascending and descending she could see lots of scattered, different-sized circles, more grey and black than coloured, representing moods, crises, hospitalisations and a few precious peaceful times of stability. The losses were heartbreakingly obvious – destroyed relationships, financial dependence, social rejection and self-loathing. Still withdrawn and curled up in the chair, Jana desperately hoped there was a way forward.

She looked up as Mary, seeing her distress, offered her an apple. Jim was wiping down the dining room tables and Anna, who was going shopping with her mum, was taking orders from all those who needed something purchased. Each was trying to help, to make a difference and prove they were worthwhile human beings. She caught my eye and spoke quietly. 'In here there is acceptance and understanding. In here I have friends. If only the community felt the same! The criticisms and the judgements are always there, making me retreat into my loneliness. I don't want to be in hospital but at least it's safe and I can be myself. As I pass people in the street I long to shout, Please don't avoid me.

You've nothing to fear. Like you I just long for friendship and a place to belong.'

Jana recalled being told that for others to fully accept her, she needed to accept herself and her limitations, throw away the guilt that was a heavy familiar burden, and stop apologising for or denying this condition that she shared with 20% of the population. She could let mental illness bind and destroy her or fight for her dignity and self-esteem. She knew that her future with her son depended on her making some positive changes, being able to see the warning signs of trouble approaching and having the courage to ask for help to cope and recover even if that meant some separations.

Uncurling herself, she began to eat the piece of fruit offered in friendship and to see this unwanted interruption of hospital as a training ground to learn new skills. It was so hard to be strong, so hard to make plans, so hard not to stress over your loved ones and the effect of your condition on their lives. She realised she couldn't do it alone and that she would need support, someone to talk to and advise her when she wasn't thinking clearly, when she was struggling with reality. Life was tough but she had to decide to make the best of it or give up. Into her mind flashed an image of Sam, the little boy that she loved passionately. She was his mum and she wanted to be a good mum.

As she gazed out the hospital window, she saw a man in a wheelchair, slowly making his way along the uneven footpath. With a shock she was reminded that it isn't only the mentally ill who face daily limitations. She imagined being blind and never knowing the colour of your child's eyes or seeing his smile. She imagined being deaf and never experiencing the joy of music and the inspiration of a symphony. Her own misery too often prevented her from seeing the big picture of many others who also suffered.

A chaplain had recently assured her that she was important to God, a worthwhile person with a personal contribution to make and a purpose to fulfil. Her soul was intact and that was a special comfort. Perhaps this made sense. After all, no one was perfect and not many are whole.

Getting out of the chair, Jana murmured to herself more than to me, 'I don't like my life but it's the one I've been given. What I do with it is up to me. If I can find a few who will take turns walking with me, encourage me and listen to my pain, laugh with me at my mistakes and not condemn when I'm unwell, I might survive. I'm not bad, just sick.' She went to find Mary, to thank her for the apple and to see if she needed anything. Jana has a message for all of us. 'When living with limits, your dreams are ripped apart and shredded. I can't bear it if you also stomp on my heart.'

Another new friend was Tammy. The minute I walked into the room, the attractive young woman stood out because of her energy and friendliness. Tammy's face lit up as she smiled and excitedly shared her plans with me. 'I'm going to go to university to become a teacher. I'm filling in the forms now. By the time I graduate, my daughter will be starting school and it will be easier for me to work and be a single mum. I love my little girl so much and need to support her and I desperately want her to be proud of me.'

For Tammy, this seemingly realistic goal may prove to be yet another cardboard dream crashing down around her and inflicting more painful bruises on her fragile self-esteem. She'd been so sure the baby's father would marry her, love her and be a soul mate. She knew she was a hard worker, honest and enthusiastic so why was long-term employment so elusive? Independent living should be easy with youth and strength on her side.

To live without a dream is like trying to fly with one wing but it's hard to get motivated and is exhausting. As I watched Tammy pick her way through the pile of disappointments, smashed hopes and broken relationships, every fibre of my being wanted her to succeed, to be accepted into university, to do well and to believe in herself and her future.

SHAPED

Along with all the others Tammy was waging a constant battle with mutilated emotions - so many setbacks, so many rejections, so few friends and so little understanding outside the walls of the hospital.

I admired Tammy's courage as she faced challenges made much more difficult by her mental illness. Ever had shoes that pinch and rub in all the wrong places? That's how it is when we try to walk in someone else's shoes as they are always uncomfortable and a bad fit but, to walk alongside with encouragement rather than criticism, empathy rather than judgement and support rather than alienation, she could maybe reach her goal. Her dreams easily topple but offering friendship could be the glue that holds her cardboard dreams together. I determined not to be part of the stream of condemnatory hot air blasting from the community that flattens all attempts at building a worthwhile life. It's another choice for being either part of the problem or the solution. A balanced mind is truly an awesome gift that we should never take for granted. Next time you bump into Tammy, enjoy her beautiful smile and meet the courageous person within. Like me, you will be inspired.

He sits immobile with a sad, grey face
alive yet trance-like and fixed
eyes that are glazed
ears permanently dazed
mind shut down, thoughts mixed.

She chatters on, endless words hit the walls
laughing, crying, so confused so trapped
body that won't rest
mind always stressed
between her and reality huge gap.

The caged clown wears many masks
hiding hurt and pain that can kill
locked in with strife
locked out from life
in the world of the mentally ill.

I have no key to unlock the cage
but pass compassion and love through the bars
to hold a hand
with family stand
seeing aching heart not deep scars.
    Caged Clown KH

_7_

In ancient times in the Middle East, pottery jars were used for storage of food and liquids but the ugliest and most misshapen were chosen to hide coins and other valuables as a thief probably wouldn't bother to look inside these.

I was about to discover more riches in secret places. It was a grey day. The rain drizzled down the windscreen as I pulled into the driveway between another pair of daunting gates and ancient buildings. Slowly I parked, observing the two-storey sandstone buildings with barred windows at Gladesville Hospital, ironically overlooking the shores of Bedlam Bay. No sun was visible through the thick cloud cover, and mist was hanging low around the grounds, a very uninviting place to be and reminding me of a haunted town.
(See photo insert page C)

The introductory course just completed had had 20 participants. Advanced Psych saw us reduced to six. As I joined the five other members of the training group, I sensed that their unspoken apprehension matched my own, even though we talked lightly of trivial things. What was I doing here?

Of course I knew why I was standing in a chronic long-stay psychiatric hospital where some of the patients were classed as criminally insane (the new politically-correct term is forensic patients). God had made it very clear that I was to be a chaplain to these wounded people and this was the next phase of that plan. I felt excited but fragile, willing but hesitant. For the first time in all my contacts with patients, I was uneasy. This place was like leaving the real world and finding yourself on a strange, forgotten planet with a different language, behaviour and dress code.

These words from Henri Nouwen as he moved from the academic setting of lecturing at Yale and Harvard to working with the developmentally disabled in a L'Arche community in Toronto, Canada, summed up my feelings too:

> *Not being able to use any of the skills that had proved so practical in the past was a real source of anxiety. I was suddenly faced with my naked self, open for affirmations and rejections, hugs and punches, smiles and tears, all dependent simply on how I was perceived at the moment. In a way it seemed I was starting my life all over again. Relationships, connections, reputations could no longer be counted on. This experience was the most important of my life because it forced me to rediscover my true identity.*
>
> *These broken, unpretentious people forced me to let go of my relevant self – the self that can do things, show things, prove things, build things – and forced me to reclaim that unadorned self in which I am completely vulnerable, open to receive and give love regardless of any accomplishments.*[2]

---

[2] Henri Nouwen, *In the Name of Jesus*, Crossroad Publishing Company, New York, 1991, p16.

Around every corner confrontation and shock swamped me and at first I was rattled to see people so much worse than Irene. No room here for complacency. I was now on a steep learning curve. The ha-ha walls here resembled moats, effective barriers that were visibly pleasing but a psychological taunting trap between residents and freedom.

Imagine being given a bunch of large sinister-looking keys with instructions to guard them very carefully and to keep a safe distance from everyone until becoming known and accepted. Working in pairs with a partner who was a tall, well-built male made me extremely grateful. What a relief! There's safety in numbers, right? The first person we saw was a young man wearing a crash helmet and the reason was immediately obvious. He was in an enclosed courtyard - rushing up and down, hitting his head on the wall, turning, and doing the same at the other end of the yard, over and over again relentlessly. Just as he couldn't stop charging, my thoughts were roaring and crashing in on me.

As I stepped deeper into this psychotic world, little did I realise that those keys would also unlock more hidden emotions and that I would receive much more than I gave. I was about to find myself, my father and my grandmother, very necessary revelations to give me a balanced understanding for this new role. Something positive was about to emerge from all the negatives including total forgiveness and finally making my peace with Irene.

As I drove back through those iron gates at the end of the first day, it was still raining. It was equally wet inside the car as I cried tears of anguish and hopelessness. I prayed for the courage to go back.

How could I show God to a 17 year old girl so abused by both father and grandfather that she may never cope in society again? What do you say to an 86 year old man who never speaks, who knows no other home than his hospital room and walled exercise yard, whose sole earthly possessions consist of a few plastic combs and a collection of scratched toy cars in a scruffy overnight bag that never leaves his side? During subsequent visits I was greatly moved to see this man smiling warmly at me and giving me a car to handle from his precious bag, sharing his limited world with me. I had become his friend although no words were ever spoken. Just being there had made a difference and I was thankful.

As the weeks progressed so did my God-given love for those trapped in a confused turmoil of ideas that refused to make any sense. Locked in with my new friends, I sensed what a frightening existence they led, and my own fears fled. Playing cricket with a plastic bat and ball was hardly gripping in its excitement, but it was a short time of fun in an otherwise sober day. Singing 'Consider Yourself' from Oliver with a patient wasn't exactly a musical highlight but we laughed together and for a few moments there was happiness. Praying with a 23 year old girl about her expected move to a less restricted ward brought a glimmer of hope and a smile to a sad, young face.

One very powerful interaction is etched on my mind forever. Phil told me I had chosen a lovely day to visit Barry. When I assured him that I hadn't come just to see Barry but everyone, tears ran down his face and he kissed me. Someone wanted to be with him. Perhaps he wasn't worthless after all. One invaluable life lesson was learning not to judge by appearances or assume without knowledge. By looking deeper below the surface I often discovered a very valid reason for a person's seemingly bizarre behaviour.

Jasmine's husband died before they had any family and she proudly showed me six dolls on her bed that she claimed were her children. 'They don't talk to me,' she confided, 'but when I'm lonely, I can touch them and they won't ever go away.' Doesn't sound too crazy, does it? There was a pottery studio in the grounds at Gladesville and I sat with Jasmine often as she tried to reshape her damaged psyche by making items for her 'babies'. The best piece I produced in these classes was a cake plate with an uneven base and a patchy blue glaze and only now am I aware that this was a mirror of my life at that point, able to be used but with imperfections and needing lots more work.

Perry was a little man with greying hair, probably between 40–50, with a very uneven gait and spittle around his mouth combined with the remains of breakfast. As we drew near each other on the path, I smiled hesitantly and said hello. He grunted, waved his arms around wildly and kept going. My first reaction to Perry was one of caution, distance and uncertainty. What to say to a developmentally disabled person who has lived in a mental institution all of his life and whose speech I couldn't understand?

Gradually over many months the real Perry began to unfold for me. Anger never seemed to afflict him and, in his limited world, he appeared happy. He never knew anyone's name but he recognised faces and remembered their connection in his establishment. He would follow me to the chaplain's office realising there was always a cup of tea and a biscuit to be begged. Often he would emerge from the kitchen grinning, with a banana and a few slices of cold meat hanging out of his pocket.

Perry was free to wander wherever he wanted and somehow never became lost and always found his way back to his room each night. I would see him sitting under a tree with a crumpled comic that he couldn't read and an unlit cigarette that he couldn't smoke hanging from his mouth. This attempt at normality showed how much he longed to belong. Later he'd be shuffling down the street with a fixed look on his face as if on an important errand but he had nowhere to go and no business to complete. What was going on inside his head? What did he think of my poor attempts to communicate?

Imagine my surprise to find Perry in church on the Sunday it was my turn to take the service at the hospital. I learnt that he came every week although no one could fathom how he knew the day and the time. Alarm set in for me as I saw that he couldn't sit still and wanted to constantly pace up and down. It was rather disconcerting to often find Perry's face almost touching mine so that I couldn't see past him. I was thankful for an active sense of humour and decided that praying with my eyes open should become the norm!

The service proceeded with minor controllable interruptions and then I finished with my final recorded song. As *Jesus loves me* was playing, my gaze was riveted on Perry. His whole body shook with excitement, he was moving with the music, clapping, and grinning so broadly I thought his smile would break through the back of his head. He sang in the same way he spoke, loud unintelligible sounds but to God I'm sure it sounded like the hallelujah chorus. So choked up was I that I couldn't sing at all.

As Perry stood there, I saw God's unsurpassed love in action. Somewhere, somehow in Perry's confused mind, he had met God and been touched by him. How little we really understand of divine influence in hearts and minds. I learnt a valuable lesson that day that will remain with me forever – NEVER ASSUME.

No one is beyond God's reach and we all hold a unique place in our world.

On another occasion while in a meeting, Perry burst through the door looking for the usual 'cuppa' and being his noisy self. He stopped abruptly when he saw we were praying, stood in the middle of the room with eyes closed and hands pressed together until we had finished. Then he quietly left, the cup of tea forgotten. He was clearly stating 'I like to worship too. I'm one with you and with our God.' No pretence here, just unity. Perry can't share his faith verbally, will never be a church worker or receive thanks for a job well done, but he has a gift of praise that I envy.

My contact with Perry began with wondering what to say and ended with the realisation that words weren't necessary. I communicated through presence, body language and an attitude of love, and God brought clarity to both of us. Discovering spiritual treasure in a clay jar was more exciting and humbling than any archaeological dig. Perry's jar was marred, unattractive and discarded but contained incredible wealth. Thank you Perry for all you taught me and for the joy of knowing you.

As a group we watched a video about Electroconvulsive Therapy (ECT) and in the debriefing session that followed, had to assess whether we would agree to it for ourselves if ever needed. It was enlightening for me as Irene had it many times when the procedure was still barbaric – immobilised on the bed with tight restraints and no anaesthetic while an electric current was applied to your head resulting in a severe convulsion. Health Department records show that 1,228 inmates are buried in the north east corner of Gladesville Hospital grounds in unmarked graves. I wondered if any of these had died from ECT and realised how tough my grandmother had been to survive her many hospitalisations in these conditions.

ECT was invented in Italy in 1938. In 1939 it was brought to England as the preferred method of inducing seizures in convulsion therapy in British mental hospitals. Although soon established as especially useful in the treatment of depression, it was also used on people with a wide variety of mental disorders. There was large variation in the amount of ECT used between different hospitals. As well as being used therapeutically, ECT was also used to control the behaviour of patients.

Although ECT is still used widely today, it has been modified considerably. It is a form of medical treatment for severe depression, bipolar disorder, and psychotic illnesses such as schizophrenia. It may be recommended when symptoms are severe or other forms of treatment are ineffective. A general anaesthetic is now given first, and then a small electric current is passed between two electrodes placed on the scalp. On waking, the person has no memory of the procedure. Treatment is typically repeated a number of times and while most people show some improvement after 3 to 4 sessions, occasionally some may need 20 to 25. Treatments are usually given 2 to 3 times a week producing an improvement in depressive and psychotic symptoms.

For some people, other forms of treatment such as medication and counselling have little or no effect on the symptoms of depression or psychosis. This is particularly concerning where symptoms are causing severe distress and the person may be suicidal. In these cases ECT seems to be especially helpful, with over 80% of people with depression who receive it reporting an improvement. Armed with this new information, I decided it could be a good thing when all else had failed. I had no idea then just how important this knowledge would be. For Dad, after Irene's experiences, it was a horror never to be forgotten and imprinted on his mind forever. He vowed he would never agree to this treatment and we were never to sign anything to that effect.

I still don't know how to answer the woman who says the police have stolen her smile. I don't have a positive, meaningful response for the man who has the key to the sun, but if I love, listen and am available perhaps a little dignity and respect will be restored to those who have lost so much. Our group of six had all struggled with how to make a difference in this environment and we all came to the same conclusion. We couldn't of ourselves change anything, but the residents were all loved by God and we had endeavoured to be a channel for that love. One thing was certain – I knew my life would never be the same.

I was so thankful for this journey that had been like stumbling slowly down a long dim tunnel, hands outstretched to gently bump into the unknown without too many bruises, and then the relief of coming out into dazzling warm sunshine. As I drove away from Gladesville Hospital for the last time, I was smiling. Finally I had put the past to rest and unlocked that part of me that had been repressed since childhood.

Now I was free to be me with new-found healthy self-worth and confidence firmly in place. Empathy and compassion for the hurting were uppermost but I had also developed an inner iron rod that poked me whenever I was put down or ignored. My grandmother couldn't help her condition and the way she related to me, but most others I meet can't use the same excuse. So be warned – my softly-spoken exterior hides a strength that will be revealed when provoked on behalf of others or for myself.

My bucket list of fun experiences began around this time and over the next few years I enjoyed taking risks as I went parasailing off Noosa Beach in Queensland, scuba diving on the Barrier Reef, hot-air ballooning over the countryside west of Sydney with my eldest daughter, and riding an elephant in Bangkok. I did manage to persuade my husband to ride a camel with me at sunset along Cable Beach in Broome, a magical experience that many have enjoyed, but when I went skydiving in Cairns over crocodile-infested rivers, he remained in the motel praying!

As I stepped through the gate at the far side of the airport, I was hit by my first slap of reality. The plane was a Cessna something or other, the pilot proudly told me, but the escalating drumming in my head drowned out his voice. There was no door and no seats, I observed, so obviously I wouldn't have to worry about seat belts! I tried to recall all the instructions I had just been given and shook my head in disbelief. The plane looked as small and flimsy as one of those you collect from a box of breakfast cereal. I realised I'd reached the point of no return, my brain was going into meltdown and total paralysis from fear was setting in.

The instructor, to whom I was now strapped, was prattling on and pointing out scenic spots below as the plane shuddered up and up, jerking in the strengthening wind. He nonchalantly commented on my white knuckles fiercely gripping the door frame. I was closest to the opening as I was going to be the first out. 'You can hang on if you wish, but I suggest you let go before your hand freezes.' As if sitting in the open doorway wasn't bad enough, I just had to hope the wind didn't suck me out. Now I knew I was mad.

My second slap of reality was that 8,000 feet really is a long way to fall, a tad further than expected. I realised with a shock that this could be the last day of my life and I prayed that I'd go with dignity without throwing up or having a more embarrassing emission from the other end of my anatomy.

'Right', said the cheerful instructor, 'just remember all I've told you, put your legs out the door onto that wheel strut and jump. Once we're clear of the wing, it will be magic.' The larger plane with the easier exit at the back had broken down, he informed me. This guy was a real comedian.

As the free fall began, so my terror started to subside. Surprisingly, rather than hurtling down through the sky, it felt as if the icy clouds were rushing up to catch and grab me, like being so close to a giant fan that you wondered if the skin on your face would be ripped off. After swinging wildly in the wind as the parachute opened, finally there was a rich quietness, both within and without, and I began to experience the magic for myself. I was alive, exhilarated and could have drifted over those lush green plantations and deceptively serene rivers surrounding Cairns forever. It seemed surreal to be floating above a silent world, exploring a distant place that until now had been out of bounds. I could taste the thrill of adventure and felt embraced by God. The landing was fairly smooth but no further skydiving was done that day because of strong winds. 'You just made it,' smiled the instructor. He asked how I planned to spend the rest of my day and with a huge grin I replied, 'bragging.'

I was very proud of myself and nothing could dampen my euphoria. I had pushed through my fear and way beyond my comfort zone, had achieved a delicious personal victory, proving there are still some untapped resources within waiting to be released, and I felt as tall as the sugarcane I'd landed near. I couldn't wait to SMS everyone in my contact list. They were going to hear every detail about my amazing experience - often - as I planned to really get my money's worth.

I removed the suit and received a certificate stating that I'd jumped on my own accord from a perfectly sound plane. Why had I done it? Probably because life is for living. Just as the plane had no door, I hope there will never be a door that I shut on my life, only new exciting opportunities through which I will continue to step. This was the most exhilarating but terrifying experience of my life. When asked by a gobsmacked friend why I did it, my reply was 'Because I could. The chance was there right in front of me and I didn't want to miss out.' Crazy? Maybe, but it was important to balance all the grief that was a big part of my life with some lighter activities.

Now you find me where I began, sitting on Irene's grave and contemplating forgiveness. The Concise Oxford Dictionary defines the word forgive as 'to let off' or 'to pardon' but it gives no clue as to how to achieve this. I discovered that forgiving is a process, realised little by little, day by day, as you confront your circumstances and slowly become willing to let go of the pain of the past and open yourself up to healing. I asked for and graciously received divine help from Jesus who said *Father, forgive them, for they do not know what they are doing* (Luke 23:34 NIV). So many in our community have huge legitimate hurts that are inwardly destroying them, repressed and festering away affecting both body and soul.

Dr Lewis B Smedes was a renowned author and a professor of theology and ethics for twenty-five years at Fuller Theological Seminary in Pasadena, California.

His books on forgiveness have dramatically changed many lives. This quote really resonated with me - *Forgiving does not erase the bitter past. A healed memory is not a deleted memory. Instead, forgiving what we cannot forget creates a new way to remember. We change the memory of our past into a hope for our future…*

To forgive is to set a prisoner free and discover that the prisoner was you.[3]

'Goodbye Irene and thanks for all you've shown me. Your feelings were out of control while, as a reaction, mine were suppressed. I grew up believing that to be strong, I had to be in control. I cried for others but denied my own emotional needs. Now I know how to get in touch with feelings in an appropriate way. Finally I am content with who I am, no longer fighting myself. When I'm driven, it's for the right reasons. If only you had been able to make that discovery also.

'I forgive you and my heart goes out to you. If only we'd really known each other, I suspect we'd have had much in common. I have your thick wavy hair, slim build and the ability to open jars that others can't budge. I was even given your name as my middle one and at last I am glad. No more resentment but a link to someone I will never forget. We share a wicked sense of humour even though yours was often silenced by your illness. Unfortunately we rarely laughed together.'

I walked slowly away knowing the past was healed and I had finally shrugged off all the negative influences that had affected me for so long. Now I knew why I had removed the jagged glass from the grave. There was no more pain. Nothing sharp or broken belonged here anymore. My grandmother had moved from being a cold name on a cold headstone to a warm regret in my heart.

'Thank you Irene for unknowingly charting the course of my life and thank you God for enabling me to make it happen.'

---

[3] Lewis Smedes, *Forgive and Forget: Healing the Hurts We Don't Deserve*, Harper Collins 1996

− 8 −

Before the glaze is applied, the piece must be prepared. First the pot is checked and any bumps or imperfections are removed. Coarse sandpaper may be used or a kitchen paring knife edge to smooth surfaces.

It's my first day as chaplain in Sutherland Hospital Mental Health Unit. My predecessor, Rev Alan Galt[4], who had been our Supervisor through all the CPE training and who taught me so much, had conducted a Pastoral Care Group each week in the ward and I was to continue with this. I believed I had something worthwhile to offer in terms of spiritual care, respect and acceptance and that I was a credible carer who could help make a difference to a patient's recovery. I had time to engage in conversation, to listen, offer comfort or simply show love by my presence. I also wanted to develop a good rapport with the staff, showing that spiritual healing can complement physical healing. My aim was to be a friend to all, in the hospital but not of the hospital. The fact that the Chaplaincy Team were all volunteers helped me to achieve this.

---

[4] Rev Alan Galt OAM, Senior Lecturer in Pastoral Theology, Level 3 CPE Supervisor, Centre Director, the Mental Health CPE Centre, Hornsby Hospital, Hornsby, NSW, Australia.

As I arrived home that day the phone was ringing and Mum told me that Dad had been hospitalised again after another eight-month-long battle with deep depression. I prayed and asked God for strength to cope with both Dad and my new friends in the hospital. Although my life had always been bound up with psychiatric disorders, now I really cared and wanted to soothe some of those raw emotions. I also wanted to be as much support to Mum as possible during the tough times even though she lived two hours away. I ached for her ongoing pain and losses and clearly recognised that I couldn't cure or 'fix' anyone but, after years of regular visits to hurting people, have found that ever-deepening empathy is a balm for troubled souls.

I ran this group for 12 years with between 4 – 10 patients attending each week. They appreciated the opportunity to discuss spiritual issues and problems for which not enough time was available in other groups they attended. The weekly program in modern psychiatric wards is busy with retraining in daily living skills, handicrafts, stress management, how to handle aggression, relaxation techniques, behaviour modification and how to deal with voices, to name a few. It's ironic that when we say we talk to God, that's usually acceptable, but when we say God talks to us, we are labelled as schizophrenic!

There is a very fine line between sanity and insanity and none of us know what events or circumstances could tip us over the edge. Mental illness is no respecter of persons and I have met policemen, teachers, nurses, young and old who are walking this very difficult path. Many are overcome with inappropriate guilt, some thinking that admission to hospital is a punishment from God. Some are encouraged when reminded that God forgives and that it is possible for a new start on release if they can let go of the guilt, shame and blame. Many asked me to pray with them, finding a measure of peace in prayer. Holding the hand of a patient and praying prior to their first ECT session eased apprehension and was an appropriate way to show God's care and perhaps help to bring about a calmer, less stressed attitude.

Some of my most difficult encounters were when I came face to face with someone from my church who was totally embarrassed and mortified at being admitted. After I promised to tell no-one and maintain confidentiality, he was grateful for this secret support and looked forward to my visits. How sad it is that we still can't accept that the brain is just another part of the body that sometimes becomes sick and out of kilter and must be cared for either in or out of hospital. I read of a Baptist minister who used to regularly visit Ward C but one devastating day walked into that same ward as a patient and couldn't leave for many months. He eventually recovered and was greatly used by God in a new church ministry, now armed with first-hand experience in fighting the exhausting psychological fiends that almost destroyed him. His empathy for others on the same journey of self-discovery and healing was inexhaustible.

It's not easy finding something to laugh at in this environment but there were times when laughter was good medicine. I remember the day Annie was curled up in bed in the foetal position and told me she was too depressed to get up because she was much sicker than she realised.

'Why do you say that?' I asked.

'Last night,' Annie continued, 'I was wide awake and alert, definitely not hallucinating, and I saw a space ship. The flashing lights went past my window and it was very noisy. I know what I saw. I'm in a bad way.'

Grinning, I replied, 'This hospital has a helipad. What you saw and heard was a helicopter bringing in a night patient.' We both burst out laughing and a relieved Annie got out of bed.

Another day I asked Ben what had happened to the gold fish. Everyone enjoyed watching them but now the tank was empty. With a sheepish grin he confessed that last week while most unwell he had given them cereal and toast for breakfast with disastrous results. We cracked up and realised how important it is for everyone to be able to laugh at themselves. These interactions have taught me to be real, to take off the masks and not to pretend. I've been sworn at and yelled at by experts with intense colourful language not heard anywhere else but I learnt so much from those who really know about tough living. The emotional outbursts from Irene that terrified Kaye the child, now gave Kaye the chaplain a window into the pain of being locked in a closed ward where others hold the keys to your future and where bizarre responses are the norm.

Part of being real for me was not giving pat answers to religious questions. These patients had heightened insights and could spot a phoney from 30 paces. They were also very spiritually aware and sometimes their illness produced an unhealthy enthusiasm, albeit often hilarious, that resulted in sermons being preached while standing on a dining room table, lounge or bed, in full voice for hours at a time. Needless to say, the staff often felt this behaviour was precipitated by the chaplain's influence so the wisdom of Solomon was required to be relevant and credible to all.

What do you say to the person who has tried to commit suicide and is furious at finding himself alive? The most difficult question I was repeatedly asked was 'Will I go to heaven if I kill myself?' At this time I completed the CPE Grief Course which proved to be invaluable both in the hospital and in life. Whenever we lose something or someone, we grieve, and I came to believe that suicide inflicted a double portion of grief on families. As well as the death of their loved one, they have to deal with the confusion and anger of having missed how much they were hurting. The 'if only' questions can leave more victims among the living.

There were only two successful suicides in the hospital during my years there. We have come to expect this outcome from mentally ill people in the community who refuse to take medication and are often exposed on the evening television news, running down the street screaming and out of control. However, the psychiatric ward is a safe, secure place of restoration and healing, and suicidal thoughts are usually picked up by doctors, psychologists and nurses very quickly. These tragic incidents came about because the patients schemed, pretended and manipulated staff into believing they were well enough for unescorted leave but both just wanted to execute a cunningly devised plan within the hospital grounds. In the shattering aftermath of distress and sadness, I had many opportunities to sit with staff and patients alike to offer comfort and love. Inappropriate guilt can destroy if not dealt with properly.

What help can you give the young mum whose kids have just been removed from her care because of her illness? And their grandparents who struggle to raise them when in poor health themselves? I had lived with family tensions but these situations are much more severe and difficult. I felt the depth of their pain and knew I couldn't remove it but by being there I showed that I cared.

I read of the little boy who, tired of waiting for the butterfly to emerge from the cocoon, finally slit it with his penknife. The butterfly's wings weren't fully formed and the boy's impatience meant that sadly it would never fly. How far will we fly without the patience and encouragement of those around us? Hope is to life what oxygen is to lungs. Without it we shrivel up and die.

It takes great courage for the mentally ill to drag themselves out of bed each day, to take medication that often produces unpleasant side effects, make decisions, go out and face a hostile world that is so quick to judge, and have enough energy to limp back home in one piece at the end of yet another frustrating and unproductive day. And I haven't even mentioned job hunting which usually falls in the category of impossible dreams! For those who make it, it is a herculean achievement.

> *Our capacity to love reaches its full maturity when we can look upon the twisted features of a fellow human being in pain and not turn away in fear or*

disgust but catch a glimpse of the suffering Christ and minister to him in all simplicity and tenderness. If we love we create, heal and release in those around us a power which seldom fails.[5]

When not in the ward, I tried to show the human face of mental illness to those who don't understand and to challenge stigma at every opportunity. I began conducting a Spiritual Awareness Group at a Living Skills Centre once a week where the attendees were recovering mental health patients, mostly male schizophrenics. The occupational therapists welcomed me and encouraged the guys to join in, recognising that any sort of assistance to cope in the real world would be positive and effectual. Being released from hospital is only the first step in assimilating back into an antagonistic and mostly unsympathetic society.

The year 1994 began with Dad readmitted and the doctors informed us that they had exhausted their treatment options. They suggested he could have ECT as a last resort. After many family discussions and much prayer, I finally convinced him to go ahead and four weeks later Dad returned home a new man with a smile on his face and we again heard the occasional song. Again God enabled me to use my new knowledge to help my own family. His depression never left and medication continued but his health settled down into a manageable pattern that kept him out of hospital in his final years.

Mum and Dad moved into a retirement village where care was available for Dad in the hostel and Mum had her own self-care unit. She was able to reinvent herself with new friends and activities and finally have some 'me' time. Mum blossomed in her new freedom to attend lunches and movies and volunteered in the Red Cross Blood Bank and the Uniting Church Op Shop, the ladies having a hilarious time trying on all the donated items. She regularly attended Bible studies and prayer meetings and we loved visiting and seeing them more settled and at

---

[5] Morton Kelsey, *Caring – How can we love one another?* Paulist Press 1981.

peace with each other. She was with Dad but no longer responsible for him and they were much happier.

While my work with the mentally ill and my pastoral care role at church were going well, life at home was unravelling. We had been experiencing financial difficulties for four years as Cliff's accountancy practice accumulated more and more bad debts due to the Global Financial Crisis. Along with many others in business, he thought he could ride it out waiting for clients to pay, but when Australia spiralled into a severe economic recession it was too late to retrieve the money owed and many went bankrupt.

It was our choice to sell the large comfortable home we owned and move into a small uncomfortable rented house to help our financial position and a rental cycle began that lasted many years. Our eldest daughter was studying at university and youngest daughter was rebelliously fighting our new living arrangements.

We lost count of the number of times, after being just a few months into a new lease, the owner decided to sell. After moving so many times, the furniture we had been able to keep was as bruised and battered as we were. Once we had two weeks until moving day and no place to go. Friends prayed and searched surrounding suburbs and God provided. One couple took their daily afternoon walk armed with pen and pad so they could record details from all signs indicating a vacant home to pass on to us. In one unforgettable week the car broke down, the frypan and toaster died and the dog became sick and needed a vet. Do you think God was trying to teach us to hold things lightly? Cliff's health deteriorated from all the stress and was hospitalised with diverticulitis, his mother died of cancer, and after years of being free to study and use my spiritual gifts in ministry, I resentfully found myself looking for work.

Cliff had been in business for 27 years, had never cheated anyone or falsified figures, honesty and integrity underpinned all dealings, Christian clients had been given regular discounts, we'd tithed faithfully and never wasted money, and both had been involved in voluntary work for over 25 years. Yes – we were hurting and confused but clinging to the knowledge that God was still watching over us and would show us the way forward. A life of service is no guarantee against problems but Cliff hadn't expected to be tested in the financial area where he felt competent and confident. We now know this often happens as God pushes us out of the warm nest to show us a new perspective and a wider world to embrace.

The Holmes' Social Readjustment Rating Scale determines the level of stress in relation to loss and claims that the accumulation of 200 or more points in one year can lead to the development of a psychiatric disorder! We were way over the 'sanity' limit yet survived. The firing was fierce as the kiln was really heating up and the following poem reflects my feelings at that time.

> *Flapping in puddles in panic*
> *from this level life is tough*
> *Lord lift my aching heart*
> *give me courage and new start*
> *help me rise above the muck.*
>
> *Soaring on high like an eagle*
> *comfortable nest lost to view*
> *Lord catch me when I fall*
> *send updraughts when I stall*
> *help me to fly, not flap, with you.*
>   To Fly   KH

Determined to continue my chaplaincy role at the hospital, I began working at Albatross Books three days a week. My job involved marketing, advertising and producing a monthly promotional catalogue.

These were the days when publishers had warehouses filled with books up to the ceiling and a fork lift was necessary to reach the top levels. In my years there, all my relatives and friends received books every birthday and Christmas and the staff, who obviously were all avid readers, often bumped into each other in the warehouse as we wandered around feeding our book addiction.

We moved our business to smaller premises with cheaper rent but every week was a struggle and financially we lived from day to day, not knowing if we'd have enough for our needs. We were one step from bankruptcy, stressed and exhausted.

Any spare time I had was spent in the office doing everything from computer maintenance, typing, filing, shredding, cleaning – in fact everything except tax returns. I had to draw the line somewhere! I am a word person who is allergic to numbers and thankfully Cliff recognised that. There was no time and no inspiration for writing during these tough years as this second firing was fierce and all consuming.

-9-

A few years later I was offered a job in the Communications Department of Wesley Mission in Sydney by Martin Johnson, the manager. We were both attending Gymea Baptist at the time and I could see God's guiding hand, especially when he agreed I could have Mondays off to continue with chaplaincy.

My role involved being the official proof reader for all printed material, writing human interest stories for *Impact* magazine, producing *Behind the Scenes*, an in-house monthly paper reporting on all aspects of the Mission that occurred on other sites outside the city. It was important for those in Accounts to know what was happening in the disability workshops; for those in Marketing to be aware of the needs of mentally ill patients in the Mission's two private hospitals; for those in Graphic Design to understand the reality of being homeless.

Rev Dr Gordon Moyes, superintendent of Wesley Mission for 27 years from 1979 till 2005, was an amazing man with gifts, vision and energy that seemed limitless to us mere mortals. He never forgot the name of hundreds of staff, knew exactly what was happening throughout every level of the building and always had time to reach out to the homeless man in the doorway or the smelly woman asking for food in the foyer. At 4.30 one Friday afternoon, I had just finished what I was working on and decided to play Solitaire for 30 minutes before leaving. Gordon hadn't been in the office all day but suddenly he appeared behind me inquiring as to how this would further the work of the Mission!

Oops – needless to say I never played Solitaire at work again. He was a writer, speaker, broadcaster, social activist, politician, prominent churchman and humanitarian, from whom I learned so much.

At the close of Gordon's two weekly radio programs, *Turn 'Round Australia* and *Sunday night Live*, he would invite listeners to write in with their problems and concerns. One of my jobs was to answer these letters. Remember that counselling course I had done years earlier?

Gordon also aired *A Moment to Think* every morning, a short thought for the day to encourage and uplift. I was asked to write these for him to record. This became the task I loved best and during my time there, I wrote over 1,000 spots. There were many days during the tough times, when sitting on the train going to work, my heart was breaking with our own difficulties and I had no idea how I could write something positive that would help others but God always gave me the right words just in time to meet my deadlines, like this one:

> *Microchipping pets is a great service. The name, address and phone number of the animal that is placed under the skin can be read from the outside and lost pets returned home. It's amazing that these tiny chips reveal so much information.*
>
> *God has put within each one of us a spirit and a desire for Him that can't be seen but is felt as we try to discover where we belong and how to find the way home.*
>
> *Microchips are a miracle of science but God's signature on our hearts draws us back from lost places to be part of His family. We have a big God with a big heart.*

What a privilege to be trusted by Gordon and empowered by God. Now I knew why I was back at work. My initial resentment at rejoining the workforce had turned to amazement at how God was using all my skills and gifts in this role that was meant for me. Everything I had ever learned had prepared me and I loved my job. I couldn't imagine spending my days anywhere else. Again God was bringing good out of bad and growing me in new ways.

Many extra things happened outside office hours that were a vital part of the Mission's program. There were regular church services with excellent speakers and Easter Sunday services at the Sydney Opera House as we watched the sun come up over the harbour. Cliff and I never missed this event and always followed it with a thoughtful walk through the Botanic Gardens.

Each year there was a memorial service for those who have lost someone to suicide, also held around the harbour foreshore. Speakers share their stories of grief and the importance of giving yourself permission to talk to others because suicide is a community issue that should not be hidden. There is always a singer or musical group who perform some sensitive songs and the clear message is that no-one has to be alone in their sorrow. One minister said, 'At its heart, the Christian message at such a gathering as this, is that God does not stand outside our experience of suffering but has entered it and shares our loss with us.' I found that really comforting.

At the end of the service, anyone who wants to can throw a sunflower into the water, both to celebrate the life lost and signify new life in the future, and a dove is released as a symbol of peace. It is such a moving moment that even those wandering past who pause to observe can't help but have a lump in their throats. There are lots of tears but counsellors are available to get alongside those who want to talk to someone. Thankfully there is now an active suicide prevention network operating in most cities and large towns across Australia that do a great job in providing vital and empathetic support to those who are vulnerable.

Then there were the fun Christmas activities like all staff being requested to sing carols out in Pitt Street in the week prior to

25th December. The majority of us who couldn't sing would fight for positions at the back where shoppers wouldn't see or hear us and many were conspicuous by their absence, having discovered urgent, unavoidable meetings they just had to attend. And did I tell you I was one of the fire wardens? Why not? Fortunately we were never needed but the regular drills as we donned helmets and protective gear and rushed down fire stairs, tumbling out onto a busy shopping mall, were hilarious.

Dad died quietly in hospital in 1999. Two days after his funeral I attended the memorial service just mentioned and although sad at my Dad's passing, was very thankful that he didn't die by his own hands. Mum had remained with him despite all the heartache and struggles, and perseverance and acceptance had finally allowed them to settle into a workable relationship.

To my father, Robert, I owe a debt of gratitude for giving me a love of the sea, learning and music that are a huge part of who I am. Swimming off my stress is still a constant release, along with lengthy walks on the beach soaking up the splendor of nature. Don't you just love sand and salt water between your toes? And the occasional rogue wave that unexpectedly drenches you? Maybe a crab's life is to be envied! My recipe for dealing with problems is first to pray then just add water. *(See photo insert page D)*

Losing myself in a good book and living in a different world for a time, or listening to classical music and allowing it to touch me on the inside where its beauty often brings tears, also helps to renew my mind, both then and now. On a recent trip to Europe I attended a Mozart concert in the Eschenbach Palace in Vienna and a piano recital of Grieg's music in the composer's former home in Norway overlooking a spectacular fjord. This was a dream come true and two experiences I will treasure forever.

Like Dad, I cry whenever I hear beautiful music. It touches something inside me. He also gave me a sensitivity to those in pain. I am really sorry that it took me so long to tell him I loved him.

When I left Wesley Mission I was contacted by Christian Television Australia. They were about to make some programs at Channel 10 called *Talking Point* hosted by Greg Gardiner where inspiring people with a faith story would be interviewed. Was I interested in finding the interviewees and then, on recording days, look after the guests and take them to the right studio at the right time? You guessed it – wild horses wouldn't have stopped me. When this program ended, I took on the same role for *Face to Face* hosted by Rev Karl Faase which followed the same format. I had made many contacts while at Wesley Mission and Cliff was also able to give me names of people he had met through his clients and ministry with various missions and other organisations. Finding enough guests for the shows was never a problem as God is always working in people's lives. I was challenged and moved as I met these wonderful doctors, policemen, musicians, writers, pastors and many ordinary Christians who with God's help, had achieved extraordinary things.

These programs were only recorded one day each month so I began *Fine Tooth Comb Copywriting and Proofreading*, an online business which began with editing theses for students for whom English wasn't their first language. Then Gordon Moyes gave me three new booklets to edit and Wesley work continued from home. I edited *One day at a time*, the story of a wife's journey through her husband's dementia and death, and was commissioned by Voice of the Martyrs to edit *Serving God in Hostile Territory*, a very moving account of the life of Bianca Adler who lived and worked in Romania and Israel during the Communist years.

-10-

Until 2005 I continued my chaplaincy work, now at two hospitals, often with bitter/sweet meetings with many who I knew well from previous admissions. They were grateful for my friendship and to see a familiar face but I was saddened that they were still struggling to cope with life in a world where they felt they didn't belong. Despite new medications and care plans, the 'revolving door syndrome' is very much alive and well, and for every mentally-ill person who does survive and succeed, despite their daily demons, many others fall between the cracks.

Is it harder to be a child with a mentally ill parent/relative or a parent with a mentally ill child? My childhood with Irene was difficult but I had no responsibility for her so was sustained by my parents' love. I was much more involved with dad's depression but was married and living away from home, not under the same roof. So many other families struggle daily with huge issues that never go away, driving them to breaking point as they keep loving and hoping for some down time, some improvement, for longer stable times and more periods of 'normal' living. A huge dilemma for parents is the sexual needs of bi-polar and schizophrenic teenagers and the unrealistic and devastating choices they often make, usually when unwell, that have far-reaching consequences to those around them.

Meeting Alison led to meeting her mum Jill, visits to their home and support over many years. Alison was feisty and determined to be independent – great qualities when you are healthy. Like all young people she longed for a partner, a loving relationship and children but these desires caused havoc. During her first pregnancy Alison refused to take her medication so her baby would not be affected by the drugs. After her daughter's birth she was so ill that she needed a long stay in hospital while Jill looked after the baby. On release, Alison took the baby to her small community housing flat, declaring fiercely that of course she could cope, but of course she couldn't. The baby was passed from mother to grandparents and back again in a continuous circle of confusion and disruption to routine.

A few years later a son was born and the problems doubled. Now there were two different unemployed dads causing trouble, aging and sick grandparents and one child ready for school. The granddaughter lived with Jill from Monday to Friday to ensure she went to school well fed and appropriately dressed and returned home to Alison on weekends. By the time the grandson started school, the granddaughter knew that nanna was much stricter than mum so refused to live with her. Simple – let's just swap things around. Now grandson is attending school from nanna's house while granddaughter, back at the flat, is manipulating Alison to allow her to stay away from school as much as possible.

There was nothing simple about it. The children were poor students with bad attitudes, often absent, always baffled as to why their lives were so different to their class mates and both with emotional baggage far too heavy for young lives to carry or understand. And of course when Alison was hospitalised and they were both at nanna's house, all their angst was directed at their grandparents without whom life would have been even tougher. You can imagine the number of government agencies involved in trying to assist these two desperate families to survive and move forward. Jill and her husband aged daily under the stress and their health deteriorated rapidly. While they loved Alison and their grandchildren, I showed love to Jill by listening, taking her cakes and flowers and driving her and her husband to appointments when she was too ill to drive herself. It was never enough, just a drop in the bucket, but never a day went by that I didn't think of them and pray for them.

With the stats revealing that one in four people will have a psychiatric episode during their lifetime, there is someone in your family, your street or your place of work who could use your help. Do you recognise this person? Mostly she's kind, helpful and willing to chat with you. However, you've noticed there are times when she wants to keep to herself, times when she seems to lock herself away and is unapproachable, times when she doesn't water the garden, clear the letterbox or answer the phone. You've heard it ringing incessantly and know she's there. Why doesn't she pick up?

Other times you've suspected she hasn't been there yet you realise she couldn't afford a holiday and she never explained her absences. Your first unthinking reaction may be to assume she is weird and to keep your distance. Who cares? Perhaps if you look beneath the surface you will discover, as I did, the demoralising illness of depression that sufferers go to great lengths to hide. As with any sickness, depression is no respecter of persons and no-one is immune. She may be a teenager, an elderly lady, a minister or a truck driver.

Those times spent in a psychiatric ward evoke a kaleidoscope of feelings in her. On the one hand she is grateful for a safe haven to rest and receive treatment, a place where for a short time she doesn't have to pretend. The masks can all be ripped off and she can reveal her raw self, be honest without fear of rejection and allow the emotional wounds to be dressed.

On the other hand, the ever-present low self-esteem, lack of confidence and inability to cope also plummet to rock bottom. 'Here I am again. Why can't I get better? I'm such a bad person.' There is encouragement in the presence of fellow sufferers, realising afresh she isn't the only one, but this is coupled with fear, the paralysing fear of having to face the world again. The old, oh so familiar tug-o-war pulls her in two directions. She longs to be home but is so scared of all that means.

When you next meet her, maybe you could try a different approach, one that offers understanding and acceptance. You will usually discover a warm, responsive person like yourself who needs companionship and who loves to laugh and share a funny story. Just as diamonds and gold need to be brought out into the sunlight to sparkle, so you may find unexpected treasure that for a little effort will make you a richer person. I've seen that sparkle many times but a sudden change of direction can make it disappear like a ring turned away from the sun. However it is there to be found by those who persevere. Do you recognise her? If not, you will meet one day soon and I hope this introduction will make the encounter a pleasant, rewarding one for both of you.

Have you made the mistake of thinking all smiling, well-dressed church goers are trouble-free? I'd like you to meet Rachel. Bent and tired she slowly trudged past, unable to lift her head or look me straight in the eye because of her heavy emotional baggage. We were in church but the sadness and helplessness emanating from her kept most people at a distance. She wasn't always like this but seemed to be pulled up and down like a yoyo on an invisible string. Up was friendly but down was flat and withdrawn.

One naïve Christian challenged her saying 'If you would only confess your sins, your load would be removed.' There are echoes of Job here! Rachel whispered, 'I've already done that many times but the burden remains.' Others suggested she pray more, read her Bible more and trust God more. She was already involved in these activities, had loved God most of her life and had a strong faith. While appreciating that the advice given was sincere and the best they had to offer, they failed to understand that these remedies weren't enough. Would anyone ever comprehend her inner turmoil and struggle that immobilised her for months at a time and drove her to self harm?

She longed for release but neither she nor anyone else could work out how to loosen this load she was carrying. She appeared to be one of those problem people that no-one knew how to handle. All attempts to help and all the advice given only tightened the ropes. There seemed to be no solution that would loosen them and ease her despair.

A few years later, to my surprise, Rachel walked past and the burden was gone. Her eyes were mostly downcast, but there was a slight smile of hope on her face and fleetingly I thought I glimpsed a sign on her back which read FRAGILE – HANDLE WITH CARE. When we next met I was excited to observe that my friend was tall and vibrant, beaming and beautiful. She appeared years younger and was obviously at peace with herself and her life. Her back was straight with no burden and no sign.

She shared with me that after a long and painful journey into the past, she had discovered that the burden was damage, and that many others in church and in the community were carrying similar unbearable loads. Many pews are sagging under the silent suffering of hurting hearts, imprisoned behind a wall of acceptable religiosity and she had been too heavy-laden herself to notice the others until now.

The damage can be made up of many things such as child abuse, abortion, rejection, neglect, smother love, divorce and destructive relationships. The burden of damage, like a crushing weight, presses down, breaking the back and the spirit and deprives of purpose and happiness.

I couldn't wait to hear the secret of this almost unrecognisable transformation. What had enabled her to untie the ropes letting the burden smash to the ground and like Humpty Dumpty never be reinstated again? This extremely difficult but life-changing process began with acknowledging that the damage wasn't her fault, walking through the years and facing the situation head on, and finally letting go of the hurt, anger, resentment, self-hatred and self-harm associated with it. Forgiveness followed for those who had inflicted the damage and it resembled digging out an embedded piece of glass without anaesthetic. So hard but so worthwhile as this was followed by emotional, physical and spiritual cleansing.

Sterilising the raw wound brought ecstatic relief from the years of agony and insured that no further infection could breed and cause harm. Liberated at last and no longer trapped.

Finally total recovery led to renewed health and peace with a scar to remind but without the presence of pain. Healing of memories gave birth to new life and a great compassion to walk hand in hand with others travelling that same dark, difficult road. With the smashing of the damage came wholeness, overwhelming relief and gratefulness to God for sustaining her through the long, weary journey. After straightening out and unravelling the past within, she could now stand tall in the present. What a journey. What a triumph.

As we strolled together in a scented garden rather than a sterile hospital, I knew that Rachel had the strength and ability to run freely into the future.

She said
too numb to feel
too tired to care
nothing to fight with
reduced and bare.
Stripped of purpose
stripped of control
nothing but darkness
surrounding my soul.

God says
I'm in the darkness
I'm holding your life

creating beauty and strength
and light in your night.
Like a fragile flower
in the wind still intact
feel the warmth of my love
and let us welcome you back.
        Held   KH

When I first met Jeff he was happily married with two cute kids, a responsible job, an active sport-filled lifestyle and a strong faith that gave him many opportunities to address groups of young people who looked up to him as a role model. He was the one who fired up the party and was popular in all circles. Life was perfect until one night while speaking at a church function, his behaviour changed dramatically. He kept talking but made no sense. He kept stopping to do push ups on the stage, and it soon became apparent that something was very wrong. Taking him to hospital was easy but for Jeff to come to terms with the diagnosis was catastrophic.

He was released and over the next few weeks couldn't comprehend or accept what was happening to him, was angry, confused and very difficult to live with. He tried to work but was suspended as being medically unfit. His wife and children moved out as they felt unsafe with his raging moods and, unable to think clearly, Jeff tried to end it all.

For the first time, at 27 years of age and at the peak of his career, he found himself admitted to a private psychiatric hospital with bi-polar disorder. When I visited him, he was tied with restraints to the bed rails to prevent a further suicide attempt and had sustained serious physical injuries that meant the sports he loved would never be played again. The storm in his soul sent thunder and lightning across the room. This was a fury I'd never seen before and words eluded me. Divorce followed. How do you dig through that huge mountain of losses and come out the other side? He was stripped of family, job, recreational activities, being a youth leader, but most shattering was the unanswerable enigma - Where was God?

It took years but his mental health improved with medication; rehabilitation and exercise enabled him to become a good golfer; he found work and began a new career and reconnected with a former girlfriend who was a nurse. They have been very happily married now for many years and her support has been an enormous help when he is unwell. In recent times he has renewed his relationship with his son and daughter much to his delight.

Why this all happened and what was learnt from it, is Jeff's story not mine, but his recovery and restored faith means that today he is often called on as a motivational speaker, loves life and loves God. Jeff probably doesn't realise what a huge impact he had on me as I watched his hard-won victory. His furnace firing at such a high temperature challenged and shocked all his friends but produced a rock-hard vessel that draws attention and will never break. He is an inspiration.

From 2000 – 2005 I edited *The Brick*, a three-issue per year magazine for Gymea Baptist Church, full of reports, special events, interesting interviews and comments on social issues. Of course you're wondering about the title. The following is my column *Perspective* in the March 2001 issue:

> *Perhaps you missed the earlier explanation of the title. No, it has nothing to do with being 'thick as a brick' but plenty to do with community – all having a place and belonging together. We are connected whether we like it or not. Each brick on its own has limited use but when many are cemented together, their usefulness is multiplied.*

A wall offers support when all around begins to crumble. Even the weakest brick will be held in place by those surrounding it. When a brick falls out or is pried loose by the jabs of a contrary theology or unaddressed hurts, the wind whistles through the holes and the wall's effectiveness is lessened. God is building us in brick by brick.

This is a timely reminder isn't it, that everyone should be helping to rebuild walls all over the world, making a difference in our little patch where God has placed us.

However, it is vital that everyone in a caring profession learns how to put boundaries in place. I now knew that I couldn't heal or fix those I walked alongside. That wasn't my role and I didn't have the skills but I could be available to many, some for only a short time, others for years, as long as I recognised my limitations and need for time out. To be swallowed up by the demands of others is to reduce effectiveness, possibly antagonise your own family and fail to be there for them. You have to fight to maintain balance in caring while trying not to neglect personal essentials or becoming entwined in inappropriate guilt when you grab a day for yourself.

A pot with an uneven base will wobble and topple, and burn-out looks a lot like a broken vessel.

– 11 –

Coloured ceramic stains and underglazes, painted on unfired white-glazed bisque, add design, decoration and beauty. Learning the best speed and pressure of the brush stroke is important for the potter.

Life was full but the potter hadn't finished. Little did I know how much more designing was still ahead but I did know that there's no safer place than in the hands of the Potter.

In 2006 Paul and I moved Mum into hostel care. At first her request seemed premature to us but as we tried to talk her out of it, she finally admitted that she could no longer understand the microwave or TV settings and it was becoming harder to cook her own meals. Accompanying her to the doctor, I was shocked at her inability to answer the assessment questions for Alzheimer's disease and we sadly accepted that now, at 85 and having cared for others for so long, she needed full-time care herself. We organised powers of attorney at her request and I took over all banking and payment of accounts. Her decline was gradual and for three years she still enjoyed bus trips, fish and chips in Nowra with her friends, playing Scrabble and knitting baby clothes for the church fete.

Although we lived in Sydney two hours away from her, we enjoyed our regular visits knowing they were about to become more difficult. Mum had always been a keen gardener and all her homes were surrounded by colourful shrubs and flowers all year round. When Natalie and Raelene were young they thought that every lovely garden was owned by a grandmother. They certainly knew that mine didn't match up!

They loved going with Mum to the pool with the waterslide and feeding the ducks in the pond in the park. However, their most-often-talked about memory was climbing through the hole in the back fence to call on a neighbour, also with visiting grandchildren, and playing housie that was rewarded with brightly wrapped prizes. These tiny trinkets were sought-after treasures and their early years with mum were so much fun.

At 88 we reluctantly knew it was time for the move to a dementia ward. Toothpaste and vitamin E cream were being used interchangeably, her phone bill tripled because of wrong numbers dialled and she could no longer find her way back to the right room. Mum was only to see her great granddaughter Zoe twice before she lost recognition but we always took her outside when visiting so we could hear the breeze rustling the leaves, admire the plants and sometimes smell the freshly mown grass. Feeling the warmth of the sun on our skin was therapeutic, a tonic for frayed emotions as we observed more and more losses.

Our grieving began then and with every visit the cruelty of this illness that afflicts so many would hit us anew. First you lose the past, then the present and of course the future. How scary to not know your name, where you are or who is caring for you. No memories, no hopes, no plans. Nothing but terrifying emptiness. The mother who had sewed so beautifully and made attractive sought-after craft items for sale, handed me her scrambled knitting full of holes and dropped stitches and I was torn apart. This I couldn't fix. Death is only one form of sorrow.

She's here but not here.
She's with me but not with me.
She's awake but not aware.

Occasionally I look up to see
Mum smiling at me –

A gentle smile
a wordless smile
a fading smile
that breaks my heart.

Dementia   KH

Content with my life and my ministries, I wasn't looking for anything new but God had other ideas.

'Have you ever thought of being a Funeral Director?' asked the voice on the phone.

My friend was looking for part-time staff to assist her and thought my previous training would be helpful. Instead of reacting and resisting with 'Not me – I couldn't do that', I prayed, reflected on how far God had brought me, and said 'Yes, why not?' As I learnt and became more familiar with the funeral industry, it became clear that the grief in the hospital as well as the grief in my new role, plus Mum's dementia, could be overwhelming if I wanted to remain focused and healthy. Part time soon became full time and I felt privileged to have input into hurting families at one of the most painful and vulnerable times of their lives. This job was both challenging and rewarding.

It was obvious that God was moving me in a different direction and I was excited. While feeling sad at leaving my friends in the mental health unit, I continued to meet with some of them over coffee and was constantly on alert for new contacts who I sensed were depressed and in need of someone to listen.

In God's scheme of things nothing is wasted and the Dealing with Grief study I had completed years earlier was again very helpful. Most of us have attended funerals but arranging one for a loved family member or friend is like berries and ferries – sounds the same but the experience is completely dissimilar. Someone once said that 'Grief is deaf' and for the person trying to comprehend an unexpected death, the myriad questions that have to be asked and the endless necessary forms to be filled in, often result in blank looks and dazed expressions.

Some can't remember what day it is, let alone their mother's maiden name and details of previous marriages, and often need a few extra days to research the family history or phone distant relatives to find answers to adequately fill in the Death Certificate application. Is the deceased to be buried or cremated? If it is going to be a burial, have you purchased a plot? If a cremation, have you thought about what you'll do with the ashes? Would you like to purchase an urn? Which cemetery or crematorium? How much do you want to spend on the coffin? Choices range between enviroboard decorated with relevant artwork that reflects the person's life through to red cedar with double-raised lid lined with pure silk. Choosing a coffin is usually the most difficult part of the whole process so must be handled with extreme care.

To proceed gently with caution worked for me, always being respectful of fierce fluctuating feelings that could break out at any moment. Church or chapel? Minister or celebrant? Funeral Directors need patience, sensitivity and compassion while asking probing questions and remaining professional. It's an emotional juggling feat that you have to get right if you want to be fit for work tomorrow and the next day and the next.

Some people wisely plan and pay for their funerals ahead of time so that they are in control of the arrangements and cost. This means that family members are less stressed when the death occurs and, in fractured families, arguments are avoided as all decisions have already been made and locked in. I recall a son whose dad died unexpectedly with no money and no discussion of these matters ever having taken place. As well as grieving, the son was furious to have been placed in the position of needing to take out a second mortgage on his house to pay for the funeral.

Raw grief hits you every day.

Every new job involves learning a new vocabulary and mine was no exception. A *first call* is the initial phone conversation where you record all the relevant information surrounding the death and begin making appointments. Did you know that *catafalque* is not a swear word but the movable platform on which the casket sits for easy transfer to chapel or church, hearse and then cemetery?

Silver knobs called *stoppers* hold the coffin in place on the tracks in the rear of the hearse. Of course I have a hearse story or two or three! Washing one is easy and refuelling at the petrol station is hilarious as observers first check to see if anyone is on board (not allowed of course) and then curiously watch as you step out of the vehicle to see if you have two heads. 'Is she mad? Surely you must be a little crazy to drive around in that.' It was hard for me to keep a straight face as I saw the expressions on their faces. Backing into a narrow driveway at the crematorium so no-one passing by would see the coffin transferred became easier with practise but maintaining a speed of 40 kilometres while driving with a deceased person in the back was always a challenge for someone with a 'lead foot' but a speeding hearse isn't a good look so I did learn.

One day I walked into the end of a phone conversation. 'They dug it where? How long will you be? Give me the address again.' Two of our men were at a cemetery waiting for a burial service to begin when the angry family arrived saying that the grave had been dug in the wrong section. They had to remain with the body until a solution was sorted out so couldn't be at the next scheduled funeral which began in 45 minutes. Sandy and I pushed aside our half eaten lunch noodles, decided that I would drive and she would navigate to St Patrick's Church, and as quickly as possible wheeled the forklift into place. Together we pulled the coffin out of the upper body refrigerator and lowered Mr Hamilton down until he was level with the back of the hearse. As my colleague rushed off to answer the phone, I pushed the coffin into place and laid his flower arrangement on top. I smiled as I remembered being told not to confuse the staff refrigerator for lunch items with this one. Cheekily I wondered if Mr Hamilton would have preferred vegemite or chicken sandwiches!

As we set off I was watching the speedometer but very conscious of the need to hurry and frustrated at the usual lunchtime crowd ambling along with their croissants and coffee and delaying us at every pedestrian crossing. Couldn't they see we were on an important mission? Then there was an ominous scraping sound from behind us. Sandy looked back and then stared at me with shock.

'You didn't' she gasped.

Feeling like a naughty schoolgirl, I confessed. 'I'm so sorry. In the rush I guess I forgot to tighten the silver thingos properly.'

'The sight of a coffin sliding from side to side is not a habit I want to cultivate' replied Sandy drily. 'Not really good for business, is it? Keep driving and let's hope no-one is paying attention.' I delivered Mr Hamilton safely, flowers still in place, with five minutes to spare, and from then on always made sure the stoppers were tightened securely. George Bernard Shaw was correct when he said - *Success does not consist in never making mistakes but in never making the same one a second time.* A sense of adventure and the ability to laugh at yourself are vital in this line of work as you never knew what a day would bring and you had to be flexible and deal with whatever situation arose with good grace and a caring smile.

Repatriation is another small word that involved a huge learning curve. Often European families wanted to send their loved one back to the homeland for burial and both the paperwork and the cost were immense. It is far easier to cremate in the country of death and return only the ashes but have you ever contemplated walking through an airport with Uncle Ned in an urn in a bag and arriving at customs? It's the stuff of funny movies but the reality is very stressful without the correct authorisation and documents.

Even more complicated is dying overseas without travel insurance. The expense, the delays, the red tape from governments with different laws and health regulations to the home country, means that often the suitcases filled with holiday mementos and photographs come back to you weeks before the body and then it's usually too late for a viewing. You hold the returned jacket you bought mum for this trip of a lifetime but you just want to see mum one more time. This is a compounded anguish for relatives waiting to plan a funeral and say goodbye.

I was constantly stretched as I began to understand the bigger picture of dying and the many layers of grief. The deeper the loss, the more hesitant you feel to invade such a personal, painful place but the deeper the loss, the greater the need to walk alongside and assist where possible. To walk in another's shoes isn't realistic – that will simply give you blisters - but by being there and offering your presence, you can make a difference. There is a cost to caring but it is so rewarding.

When asked to go and find a box of *NEFs* in our storeroom, I was nonplussed. When told that meant Natural Expression Formers, I was still none the wiser. Now I know that after death some people have sunken jaws or missing dentures so these plastic mouth plates are inserted to create a fuller face. Often we look better in death than in life which helps relatives to cope with their distress when there is a viewing. The exception was William. The nursing home couldn't find his dentures so, thinking they were helping, inserted in a spare pair. We prepared him for the viewing and the family arrived to find him grinning at them through oversized teeth that prevented his mouth from closing. Seeing he hadn't worn his teeth for months, they were horrified at his clown-like appearance. The moral of the story – if you reside in a nursing home, have your initials engraved on your dentures.

There was a deceased lady whose daughter had just arrived from her home in Scotland. She hadn't seen her mum for six months and needed to say a final goodbye but needed me to take her arm and accompany her to the open coffin in the chapel. Most people find it really difficult to look at a dead body but your loved one looks so peaceful that it's not a scary experience. It's a much better last memory than how they looked in hospital with all those tubes attached or the gruesome sight at an accident scene! This woman's dentures didn't arrive with her clothes so we inserted NEFs. The daughter was pleased at her mum's appearance but asked me to comb her hair a different way as the mortician didn't get it quite right. This was a first for me but it was all part of the job and I was happy to help her have a better memory to take with her.

A really sad viewing was a 14-year-old boy who died of cystic fibrosis. I glanced outside to see a group of boys in school uniform standing on the footpath, trying to look brave but too terrified to come in. I encouraged them and explained that it was a lovely thing to do for their friend even if there was really hard. Slowly his friends filed past, placing cards and other mementos in the coffin to go with him. Eventually only his family remained, overwhelmed to see their son covered in these gifts of love and no longer gasping for breath. Finally he could rest.

There was the time a boy wanted to put his goldfish, swimming happily in a fishbowl, in his grandfather's coffin. After we explained that neither glass objects nor any liquid could travel with the deceased, the boy became very distressed. Without promising to do as he asked, we agreed to find a workable solution and asked him to trust us to do the right thing. There were only two options that we could think of – take the fish out of the bowl and put him in the coffin to die, or let him live and draw straws as to who would take him home. Although we went to great lengths to satisfy and respect the requests of families, in this case we opted for the latter and were very thankful there was no viewing. It was both funny and moving and we were often conflicted. Do you laugh or cry? Stay strong or weep together?

Some days are more difficult than others. I had to take a still-born baby to the home of the parents for a final viewing. I kept looking at this precious cargo in the tiny white coffin on the front seat of the hearse beside me. The house was full of grieving relatives who watched as I removed the lid to reveal little Carmen looking like a beautiful doll in her tiny specially-made dress and without a mark on her. She seemed perfect. Like an angel. It tore me apart to have to tell mum that she couldn't cuddle her baby girl as her skin was too fragile to be handled but could only kiss her and gently hold her hand. I drove away for an hour feeling the brutal weight of their sorrow. On my return, I settled the parents in the back seat and placed Carmen's coffin on her dad's lap. They sobbed all the way to the church.

During the service the parents both read a poem that they had written to say goodbye to this much loved and long-awaited child. There wasn't a dry eye in the crowded church. Then I drove them to Karinya, the children's section at Woronora Cemetery, with dad still holding the coffin. The plaque at the entrance to the garden says:

> ***Fleetingly known yet ever remembered.***
> ***This is your child now and always.***
> ***These who we see not, we will forget not.***
> ***Lives that touched our lives tenderly, briefly***
> ***Now in the one light living always.***
> ***Named in our hearts, now safe from all harm.***
> ***We will remember all our days.***

It's hard to believe that no-one knows who wrote that. It's so meaningful but the author is unknown. Despite the naked heartache emanating from the mourners, this was the most disturbingly peaceful place I have ever visited. Surrounded by leafy trees and hedges for protection, scented bushes and flowers all make this botanical garden live up to its name – Karinya is Aboriginal for happy home. Teddy bears, toys and wind chimes are present everywhere, keeping vigilant watch over their young charges. Then, trying to remain calm and professional, I drove the parents back to their house where neighbours were waiting with refreshments. By the time I got back to the office I was exhausted and emotionally wrung out.

Funeral directors sometimes appear stiff and unfeeling but it's a coping mechanism that hides the gut-wrenching reaction inside. No-one remains unmoved at a child's graveside as doves or butterflies are often released to try to soften bereavement with beauty. The butterfly has long been the symbol of freedom and new life or the beginning of a new journey while some send their love on the wings of a dove. Our mortician, who was a dad himself, took extra care with children and babies, empathising as if they were his own, often working late to make sure he did the best job possible.

Another lady had two white Maltese terriers that were like children to her. They were brought into the chapel wearing red ribbons on their collars by her son. They plopped down in front of the catafalque, heads on paws, and didn't move. It was as if they knew Beryl was in the coffin and they wanted to be near her. Again it was both beautiful and sad. I had to keep my eyes off them or I would have broken down.

Suicides are particularly difficult as they bring an extra grief. Along with the normal sorrow and feelings of loss, there is anger and guilt. 'How did we miss this? Why didn't he talk to someone? How could he do this to us? Will we ever understand the reason?' Because all suicide victims have to be taken to the coroner for an autopsy which delays the funeral, this adds another thick layer of distress to already unfathomable heartache. That was always another tough conversation to have with shattered families, plus the possibility that a viewing may not be wise even though they desperately need to say a final goodbye. 'Better to remember him as he was' doesn't sit well with bereft parents left empty and confused as they struggle for answers they'll never find.

A man serving time in the local prison wanted to attend his father's service in our chapel. He arrived in a windowless van in his prison uniform. The guard to whom he was attached at all times escorted him to our bathroom where he changed into street clothes provided by his family and a cloth was placed over the handcuffs in an attempt to disguise the situation from everyone present. As soon as the last song was played, he was ushered away to change again and then hurried to the van without being allowed to socialise even for five minutes. The atmosphere was more sombre than usual and brought home to all of us how a death often brings to light deep family secrets that have formerly remained hidden or not been resolved. A funeral can either bring about renewal and healing or open the wounds afresh and then bury them even deeper.

The Archbishop was late. Over 200 mourners packed the church and the service was due to start. Then came the call. 'I'm stuck in a huge traffic jam in the cross-city tunnel and have no idea how long it will take to clear.' The four staff members present all started ringing their contacts in the area to find a fill-in minister of the same denomination who could change into something appropriate, drive fast, remember all the details of the deceased that were being read out to him and plan what to say. It was a big ask but a wonderful man agreed and, if filling the shoes of the Archbishop was daunting, he never complained. Then one of my colleagues had a bright idea.

'As you're the religious one here Kaye, you can make the announcement so everyone knows what's happening and then read the Bible or something to fill in the time.'

Or something? After explaining the delay, I was about to suggest a thoughtful walk through the beautiful garden outside when our rescuer arrived. He began the service and 20 minutes later the Archbishop arrived to complete it. The guests appreciated the dual involvement and we were extremely grateful to the minister who had so graciously risen to the occasion.

Life used to be a mystery until God gave me direction and purpose. Am I a really strong person? No way, but I've discovered how an amazing God can take a weak but willing follower and empower with courage and mental strength to do things that were previously impossible. I have proved over and over the truth of 1 Thessalonians 5:24 (NIV) – *He who has called you is faithful and he will do it.* The design on my vessel was gradually being applied.

−12−

There were many meetings behind closed doors and we knew something was afoot in the funeral industry. It was 2010 and we were informed of an ownership change that meant shuffling of staff between branches, often involving longer travelling time, new procedures and computer programs and, as always happens in these situations, there was much dissatisfaction and uncertainty regarding job security. I had been thinking for some time that when I left I would like to become a funeral celebrant so that I could continue to help people in their grief and still use the knowledge I had gained. Now was the right time.

After attending 3-4 services every week for years, I knew what not to say as I listened to the feedback from other staff members – 'Too long, too boring, didn't understand a word he said'. And the positive comments such as 'I'm not a believer but he seemed to be in touch with God and it was a beautiful service'. My already established contacts meant that work came my way easily once I let my new role be known and it grew as time went on.

All writers accumulate meaningful printed material and I already had a substantial collection of prayers, poems and other readings that I had been gathering all my life. Could they be for such a time as this? My former boss at Wesley Mission would have chuckled to know I was now writing eulogies on a regular basis. Many mourners find it extremely difficult to put their loved one's life on paper, struggling to remember the chronological order of events long passed and to express deep feelings that often had been repressed for years. It was a privilege to listen to their stories then write a tribute that was both a record to present at the service and then to keep to be passed on to younger generations.

Because God was at work behind the scenes, everything fell into place seamlessly. My work as a hospital chaplain and as a funeral director gave me valuable insights into the lives of the families I met and a deeper empathy and understanding of their needs. My love of words enabled me to choose appropriate readings for different circumstances and, as the work was part time, not be overwhelmed by grief.

Two services in particular stand out. The first was a 97 year old lady who, over her long life, had alienated everyone who knew her with her acidic tongue and mean- spirited attitude. There were to be no Bible readings or prayers, no poems that mentioned love or being missed, nothing about happy memories and of course no-one was willing to prepare or read a eulogy. That suggestion brought loud scoffing and derision.

I gulped and said, 'There is really very little left for me to use and this will probably be the shortest funeral in history.'

I was so saddened by the family's response. 'We will still go ahead because even though no-one wants to be there, it is the right thing to do. We're doing this for ourselves, not for her. We can't forgive her but our consciences are clear. We will give her an appropriate send-off and do what is required.' Music was all that remained for me so my challenge was to find five very long songs, instead of the usual three short ones, with bland, nondescript words devoid of all emotion. Amazingly, the six relatives who attended, the only mourners present, told me afterwards that the service was exactly what they wanted. How could I be pleased with that? I drove home with a very heavy heart praying that something in my presence or presentation reflected God.

What a challenge to live well and be remembered lovingly rather than leave bitterness and anger as a poisonous legacy.

The second service was for a three year old boy who was cherished by his family for his beautiful personality that radiated love to all. The chapel was full and overflowing 30 minutes prior to commencement, most friends being young parents themselves and empathising painfully as they clutched their own babies close. The level of grief was deeper than any I'd experienced before, an overpowering smothering tsunami, made even harder to bear as mum could be heard wailing and moaning outside before being almost carried to the front row by her husband and father.

Surrounded by colourful balloons, teddies and toys I began, so grateful for a group of friends who were praying for me. The overhead photo presentation and accompanying music, all favourite songs the little boy loved to sing, was heart-wrenching as we relived his all too few Christmas and birthday celebrations, saw his infectious smile again and again beaming down on us, and heard his innocent giggles. Normally the laughter of a child is pure delight. Today it was agony. The poem I had practised many times caught in my throat and tears fell. The celebrant is the one usually looked to for strength on these occasions but I recalled that a tear is 1% water and 99% feelings and knew my audience understood another mother's heart. The first part of the service concluded.

Now, imagine if you can, a very large crowd of people walking sombrely in the rain under grey skies and dripping umbrellas to the open grave site, and a small white coffin being lowered to a place where the parents can no longer accompany it. The raw pain and anguish visible on all faces is still with me. It had been a long apprenticeship, but now I was emotionally mature as well as physically mature and could deal with my feelings in a healthy manner. It's very important to develop both aspects of our lives in order to be more useful in serving others. On arriving home I sobbed the remainder of my tears for this broken family and then fell into an exhausted sleep. Waking refreshed, I knew that out of devastation grows strength. Only God. Only God.

At the time of writing, I have conducted 90 services for men and women, young and old, cremations and burials, and my work is ongoing. This is an unusual ministry but a wonderful opportunity to be a channel of his love to hurting people who may not have ever thought about the one who holds life and death in his hands and is the comforter in all of life's tragedies.

Having been too busy to write for some time, I now had a burning desire to use all the ideas I had stuffed into folders and finally work on the novel that had been a high school dream. I also now had years of life experience to draw on. The jigsaw pieces of my earlier life had clicked into place and I was humbled to realise that divine timing is always perfect and that with God, nothing is wasted. Although a long time coming, my manuscript would now have real characters with real problems but with faith and laughter to cushion the blows. I had learnt quickly that without the ability to laugh at ourselves, life can suck us dry.

So Book 1 began as I included my love of animals and many of the special encounters that had helped form the fabric of my life. Dismayed, many friends rang to ask if they would find themselves within the pages, but while the feelings are authentic, the characters and situations are not. *Dawn of Hope* was published in 2013 and the back cover explains:

> ***From hospital to hope,***
> ***from brokenness to wholeness—***
> ***could it happen for her?***

In Sydney, Australia, in the 21st century, it is still difficult to be different. Despite anti-discrimination and equal opportunity laws, there are social stigmas firmly in place and Toni is fighting for survival. Will her secret have to remain hidden forever?

Falling in love with her sister's boyfriend is her first obstacle, and coming to terms with her father's death unpacks some surprising revelations.

Working with animals is more rewarding than competing with humans and throwing herself into her job provides humour and light relief in her world of struggle and misunderstanding.

But Toni soon realizes she wants more from life. She wants love, an enduring relationship and a meaningful future. As she explores faith and loss, self-acceptance and purpose, she takes us on a heart-warming journey through sadness and doubt, mirth and elation, to unknown possibilities.

Kept by Love, the sequel, was published in 2014 and continues the story:

As her perfect world begins to crumble, can she find strength to cope with dashed hopes and shattered emotions?

To accept yourself, like what you see, and acknowledge that others like what they see, had been a long process for Toni. For over a year she'd been basking in the warmth of being married to the man of her dreams and working in a new career she loved, but vulnerability and uncertainty were never far from the surface.

She couldn't know that someone unexpected would enter her life, revealing hidden secrets from the past and neither was she prepared for established norms to irrevocably change and be tested.

Being married meant learning to communicate at a deeper level, sharing plans and goals, and she begins to question life and belief. What did she have to contribute? How do you move forward during the tough times?

As we journey with Toni again, we share her laughter and tears as she tries to balance doubt and faith, loss and blessing, sadness and joy. Will she lose herself in the fight to survive or discover what really matters in life?

My platform and brand for writing has always been to encourage and guide hurting people through difficult times, to walk alongside them on their often misty journey with no clear destination in sight. This is such a privilege and we have both been blessed as we travelled together.

My website www.kayehollings.com and my business card also follow this theme of OUT OF THE STORM.

Why did I choose fiction?

An article in the *Sydney Morning Herald* on 6 January, 2014 by Mark O'Connell, says it better than I can.

**A scientific fact:
reading fiction is good for the soul.**

...But to make any headway with a novel, you need to grant yourself a leave of absence from human affairs, to sequester yourself in a place where you are sheltered from the demanding presence of other people.

...The consensus among writers has generally been that imagining ourselves into fictional minds and lives is something that increases our moral faculties, a practice that grows our capacity for empathetic engagement with the minds and lives of actually existing other humans. Novelists have historically tended to be invested in the notion that narrative art can jolt us out of selfish complacency. [6]

My choice of inspirational fiction as my genre has been justified in that both men and women, young and old have related to and enjoyed Toni's struggles, and have laughed and cried with her. It's hard to describe the joy of finally having two titles published and of receiving positive feedback. It's been fulfilling, exciting, immensely satisfying and also humbling to realise that despite my impatience and grumbling, God had everything under control.

---

[6] Mark O'Connell is a postdoctoral research fellow in the School of English, Trinity College, Dublin.

−13−

The next stage in the creation of the pot is the application of glaze. Every potter has his or her own formulation for glazes and many of these are a closely guarded secret as the unique properties imparted by a particular glaze, fired on a particular clay body, combined with the characteristics of the design of the piece, are what identifies the pot as belonging to a certain potter. Once the pot is glazed, it is returned to the kiln for a second firing, in which the clay and the glaze are matured, meaning stoneware is brought to a temperature at which it is no longer porous and the glaze achieves a glasslike finish.

Glazing is probably the most challenging part of making pottery. It takes a lot of practise and experimentation to get it right and it is easy to ruin a successful pot by getting the glazing wrong. The Master Potter doesn't make mistakes even though I was often resistant to his fashioning.

Although my writing was going well, that was not the case in my personal life and I began to think God had forgotten us. Our girls had moved to Queensland many years ago and we knew that on retiring, we would also move to the Gold Coast to be nearer them and our grandchildren. For a long time the burden of debt had been crippling but now, instead of limping along, we could stride ahead and make plans. We moved house again and Cliff placed his accounting practice on the market in 2011. A suitable buyer emerged and was at first very keen, then procrastinated, then didn't proceed. Big disappointment. Nothing happened for 12 months. Early in 2012 four more potential buyers fell through. Even bigger disappointment. So we faced another new year with no answers and no clue as to how to move forward. We were trying to trust in the dark and kept falling over our fears and uncertainties and each other. I was constantly being hit in the face with the reality of Proverbs 13:12 (NIV) – *Hope deferred makes the heart sick.*

Needing an uplift, we attended a service at Canaan of God's Comfort, an interdenominational centre at Theresa Park, west of Sydney, surrounded by peaceful farms, calming countryside and space to think. This refuge from the relentless rush of life is run by the Evangelical Sisters of Mary, an order of Lutheran nuns dedicated to studying the Bible, prayer and reaching out into the community. They offer retreats, conferences, chapel services and guided quiet days where you are given themed questions to focus on, then dispersed throughout the grounds to spend time in solitude and reflection.

It was Easter and we discovered their Prayer Garden representing the Via Dolorosa or Way of the Cross. Here we spent time praying and reflecting as we slowly walked through the seven stops made by Christ on the way to his crucifixion, depicted by meaningful Scriptures etched in stone, statues, water features and hanging plants. Despite the horror of that sacrificial journey, we could now ponder its earth-shattering significance in undisturbed peace and quiet. As we drove home, our circumstances hadn't changed but perhaps that moving experience would refresh our souls and strengthen us for the long haul. I was very grateful for this haven for hurting hearts.

The stone was rolled away.
My fluctuating faith
my stress
my mess
rolls it back in place.
The rock
can still block
access to him.

The stone was rolled away
from my dark place
from tears
from fears.
I'll flee the clutching shadows
with your power
me endow.
Let miracle dawn daily in my heart.

The stone was rolled away.
Help me run boldly into the sunshine.
Rolled Away   KH

And so as 2013 arrived, it didn't look promising. The business hadn't sold despite many nibbles that never came to fruition and we moved yet again as owners kept deciding to sell just after we had signed a new lease. This was our eighth move, eight lots of scratches and dints on furniture, eight changes of addresses and phone numbers, being unsettled and impermanent. Years earlier friends had begun writing our contact details in pencil! If nothing else, we learnt to hold our possessions lightly and that our security and roots were in God alone. He knew where we belonged even when we didn't. Then both girls lost their homes through a failed business venture and as history repeated itself, we were shell-shocked. How could this be happening again? Mum now couldn't walk or talk and no longer recognised us. After seeing her, I would often drive home blinded by tears of memories of who she used to be. Could anything else go wrong?

Worn out, stressed and confused became the norm. One of my diary entries at this time said, 'We are still trying to trust and believe that God has a plan and an end to all this, but we feel attacked on all sides and I've certainly lost my sense of humour!' Oh for some good news. At this point I was pleading with God – 'Please leave me alone. I don't want to be worked on any more or learn any new lessons. It's too hard. Just let me sit and rest. Stop glazing. It's too painful and too hot where you have placed me. Let me remain an unadorned vessel.'

Selwyn Hughes wisely observed that God often reveals, reverses and then restores. Along with us, many have experienced a reversal in their situations and a longing for restoration. As we approached Easter again, I was praying for a resurrection of hope but instead received a deluge of setbacks. In October 2014 Cliff was diagnosed with prostate cancer requiring immediate surgery. How did this fit with selling up and doing the final move to Queensland? Why now? How would I cope if he died and I had to navigate through all the paperwork, legal documents, payment of staff entitlements, etc etc. And don't forget I knew nothing about such financial arrangements. I was always the word woman married to the numbers man.

Recovery was painful and difficult but Cliff was back at the office doing half days just three weeks after surgery because the accountant who had first contacted us four years earlier rang to say he was now in a position to buy, was still very interested and would be in touch shortly. I was now working full time in the business as the pressure was on to complete work in progress, prepare our seven staff members for coming changes, and overall, try to encourage Cliff and keep him coping, while driving him to doctors' appointments and fitting in visits to Mum. There was no time to write or take funerals. A sale offer was made and accepted in January 2015 with settlement aimed for July.

After such a long wait, we had hoped and prayed that the buyer would continue on in our existing office but it wasn't to be. Staff and all client records had to be transferred to the new location and we had to stay another three months for Cliff to expedite client handover and completely empty our very large office. This became even tougher when more cancer was found and new treatment needed.

We began the mammoth task of shredding 20 years of archived files, tried to sell off or give away furniture, dismantle shelving and paint throughout. That year I gained a Master's Degree in shredding! Have you tried to sell office equipment recently? In Sydney in 2015 no-one was interested. Twenty seven high steel cupboards had to be carried down a long flight of stairs, along with filing cabinets and all metal items. All wooden desks, bookcases, shelving and chairs were chopped up with an axe and dropped out the window into the truck waiting in the laneway below. It seemed such a waste but even the charities didn't have a need for these things. Paul and his truck were a godsend, making so many trips to the tip that the truck could find its own way there without a driver.

On the positive side, those last four years saw increased growth in the business resulting in a much better sale. Cliff could have sold the practice many times over but would only sell to someone who had the same ethics and principles as over 50% of our clients were Christian – churches, pastors, missionary organisations to name a few. He was also very thankful that all our staff were retained by the new owner. This was really important to us as, after being faithful employees for many years, they were like family and we would have been distressed if they were out of work.

Of course we were thrilled that the sale was finally happening, but couldn't it have been easier? In the midst of tiredness, aching muscles and dust, we also had to find time to go to Queensland to buy a house and pack up our existing home. The joy I had expected when we eventually arrived at this point was deadened by exhaustion.

I spent hours contacting real estate agents with our requirements giving the strict proviso not to show us anything that was out of our specified area or price range. We were on a mission and totally focused and, as the flight took off from Sydney, we were beginning to feel excited. We had only allowed ourselves 10 days to search, purchase and organise everything due to the pressure of time and amount of cleaning up still to be done. Off the plane we rushed, into the car with GPS fired up and a back-up map in case our vocal travel assistant fell off the grid, to first house inspection in one hour.

On the fourth day we found it – right size, right suburb, right price, surrounded by lovely gardens in a secure complex with a gym and pool for destressing. When God eventually moves we often have to run to keep up and we ran gladly through the rest of that unforgettable week, measuring, planning, signing, more measuring and with absolutely no doubt he had hand-picked our new home. Ever seen energetic exuberance? That was us – grateful, stunned and so relieved that we could now plan a new future in our own home with our faithful unchanging God beside us.

On the way back to the airport we stopped to order a new bed and a new oven. No point beginning the next phase of your life if you can't sleep and eat, right? There were some hiccoughs and delays with settlement and our plan to finish the jobs at the office with a clear week to pack up our unit went awry. The night before the removalist truck arrived, we finally locked the door at 5 pm for the last time. We'd been trying to sell my car for weeks in order to drive only one vehicle interstate sharing the driving, but the 'sure' sale fell through at the last minute. So we now drove to Paul's house, leaving the car for him to sell, along with the shredder. Although I had a love/hate relationship with this machine and never wanted to see one again, we couldn't justify also throwing this out the window. Now we dragged ourselves home to finalise the last of our boxes.

The two-day drive north was wonderful as we sat and soaked up the scenery, daring to relax a little with no work to do – just get there. We arrived to find that although the painting, carpet cleaning and repairs had been completed as we had requested, there was a large pile of wood cuts, broken shelves, plastic wrap, wire, screws and other assorted junk staring up at us from the middle of the lounge room floor. Too tired to deal with it, we returned at 6am the next morning, piled the rubbish outside, and by 7am when our furniture truck pulled up, we were beaming with anticipation at the prospect of unloading our future.

On arrival at our new home there was a lovely bunch of yellow roses in an elegant vase smiling at us from the kitchen bench, the perfume gently following us as we worked. In the midst of our tiredness and all the tasks still to do, this gift from our daughter Raelene was like a ray of sunshine that energised us to keep going. My prayer is that, when life slows me down, my pot can brighten rooms with his fragrance of love that pervades and uplifts sagging spirits.

Our doorbell didn't work and grandson Tyler was most concerned and questioned us every time he came. Finally we replaced it but the setting was wrong and it kept ringing when no-one was there. Cliff told him it was a new toy for the geckoes that scrambled over the walls and he thought that was very cool! Makes sense to me!

It took several months for us to slow down physically and longer to slow our minds into allowing us uninterrupted sleep with trouble-free dreams but we were home and overjoyed! Trust and surrender is the only way to survive.

SHAPED

Seagull flailing
   seagull failing
   against the wind.
Seagull tiring
seagull striving
against the wind.
Slowly turning
strength returning
helped by wind.
Like the gull
when all seems lost —
change direction.
Surrender KH

-14-

The Divine Potter doesn't discard unresponsive and stubborn clay as others might. He continues modelling and reworking until we are fully sculpted and ready to be used. His careful and meticulous preparation ensures a strong, long-lasting product. Only unfired objects are liable to break.

Now what? Our first year was spent settling in, finding our way around, exploring our new state, settling into a new church and making many wonderful new friends. Definitely a brand new start and I'm still laughing! We are revelling in the nearness of our daughters and grandchildren, and love the school holiday sleepovers with swimming, movies, feeding ducks and turtles, and playing games. We have even added a Brisbane Monopoly board to our collection! I'd love to share all this with mum so she could see the circle of life continuing but it's not possible in her advanced stage of dementia.

Now 95, she has been lost to us for seven years. Mum's lifetime example of perseverance and faith in God to overcome adversity has given Paul and me an unforgettable example on which to build our lives. We have tried to emulate her generous spirit that kept on giving. Mum always looked out for everyone else's welfare and seemed to receive very little in return. Personal rewards were few but her impact on the lives of her children is deep and ongoing. Her life was full of losses but she gave us a legacy of caring for others, a love of gardens and flowers and so much more.

On 10 March, 2017, the phone call came and, as mum went to her eternal home, she was at last able to peel off the strangling dementia and run freely into the arms of Jesus, healed and whole. Now she'll observe from a heavenly perspective and with memory restored, rejoice with us.

My earlier poem called 'Dementia' now has extra verses and a new title:

CELEBRATION

She's here but not here
she's with me but not with me
she's awake but not aware.

Occasionally I look up to see
Mum smiling at me.

A gentle smile
a wordless smile
a fading smile
that breaks my heart.

Now she's not here
but still with me.
She's awake in His arms.

Occasionally I look up to see
Mum smiling at me.

A glowing smile
a knowing smile
a loving smile
that explodes my heart.

There has been time to write this book, we're currently on the Pastoral Care team at Mosaic Baptist and I'm part of the mentoring team. I'm also still conducting funeral services for those who have no contact with a minister or priest, and am humbled by ongoing opportunities to try to make a difference and reflect God's love.

Just three days after mum's death I was contacted at 12 noon and asked if I could take a service at 2pm. No pressure – what to say, what to wear, do I have time for lunch, is it a bad hair day? The arranged celebrant had been taken to hospital suddenly and the family were distraught and panicking. Their mum had died the same day as mine and she was also a much loved lady. The old Kaye would have said 'No way' but in my spirit I knew there was an unknown reason why I should be there for this family and that God would again give me his strength to rise above my grief and help them deal with theirs.

There was a lot of prayer in the next two hours as I rushed around preparing! This was God in action and of course he came through for me. The family was extremely grateful and commented it was just the sort of service they wanted. Thank you Lord for enabling me to focus on them and their needs and for giving me the right words at short notice. Life is busy, we are content and know we are where we're meant to be.

'Made for more' was the theme for a women's retreat I attended recently. Those three small words are profound and should reverberate with all of us. No matter our age, our health, our family situation, there is always something useful we can do to grow our inner life, even if our service is limited or modified through circumstances.

Being more involves surrender. We surrender our will for him to fashion, we surrender our families, children and finances into his care, and we surrender to his timing, eventually realising that there's something to be learned in the waiting and that patience has to be earned not bestowed. I waited long years for my parents to find God;

long years before writing for radio; long years for a published novel; and more long years for the sale of our business. Despite the testing, my stressed impatience, and often a crushed spirit, God knew what he was doing. Although stretching and trying, delays are the potter's drying times before firing begins and crucial to the finished product. Delays contribute to the deepening of each person's unique and intricate design. We are made for more so let's not settle for less.

Images and metaphors about pottery are all around us especially with the resurgence of handicraft classes and exhibitions. We hear of being shaped by circumstances or formed by experiences. Someone will carve out a place for himself while someone else may become clay in unfriendly hands. After a really bad day we may be shattered or thrown by what has happened.

> Selwyn Hughes reminds us: ...*As Christians we can be too easily lulled into thinking that our faith is there to construct comfort zones for us into which we can snuggle, protected from a dangerous world. Too often we simply want to be looked after and kept safe – in other words, we want to be cosseted and pampered. This attitude is a far cry from that of the first Christians, for whom faith was bracing and life a challenge...*
>
> *...Focus now on what we have to do in order to bring our personalities back into correspondence with the divine design and thus ensure that our souls do more than survive but thrive...Don't be satisfied with the mere duties of the Christian life...Only in a passionate relationship with God will your longings for security, self-worth and significance be met...*[7]

After taking a burial service recently, I received a card which said:

---

[7] *Every day with Jesus*, March/April 2016, He died climbing!
Every day with Jesus, January/February 2016, Lacking in passion

> **Dear Kaye**
>
> *We just wanted to say thank you for looking after us so well with the funeral service for my husband. Your professional approach, warmth and compassion was evident throughout the whole process. It was a beautiful service and your words and readings were just what we were looking for. You eased the burden for us during this difficult and sad time. Your efforts were so appreciated.*

Only God could take a self-conscious girl and turn her into a capable, confident woman. Yes, I gladly took the service but he touched their hearts by sending a subtle fragrance through me that was a reminder of his presence and an invitation to explore further. *But thanks be to God who through us spreads everywhere the fragrance of the knowledge of him.* (2 Corinthians 2:14 NIV)

William Newton Clarke (1840-1912) was a Baptist theologian and famed professor at Colgate Theological Seminary, USA. He has been published widely in academic circles but his paraphrase of 2 Corinthians 5:7 has captured the minds of people all over the world in the form of inspirational posters and artworks of spectacular scenery overlaid with these words -

FAITH IS DARING THE SOUL TO GO BEYOND WHAT THE EYES CAN SEE. I have experienced that. Have you? It is life changing.

Only God could place my unwilling clay in his hands and mould, squeeze and stretch until the shape was right. Pottery is very messy but gloves are never worn as the potter must be able to feel the texture of the clay. It's very much a hands-on procedure.

Only God could turn my inadequacies into a useful life, uneven and unbalanced no more. He saw my raw potential and mixed the past with the present to form a new identity that enabled me to say, along with Ethel Waters, the soul-stirring singer, 'I'm ok 'cause God doesn't make junk.' Don't you love that? Woo hoo! I am confident that my pot won't crack but with the advance of time and old age, its uses may become less.

We see the imprint of God's craftsmanship in the incredible world he created and also in the inner world of transformed lives that have been chiselled and refined.

We are the clay, you are the potter; we are all the work of your hand. (Isaiah 64:8 NIV)

Come with me for a stroll around the pottery workshop. You may see yourself on the wheel at the start of your shaping, an exciting place to be. Perhaps you're ready to have the excess clay trimmed off to give balance, impurities dug out and base completely centred. It if won't stand up, it has to be remade but there is no limit on how long it takes or how many times it is reworked. Having waited the right amount of time for the pot to dry, some are ready for bisque firing. The shelves are full of these items that are incomplete but with such raw potential.

We move into the room housing the kilns. After firing at around 1000°C there's another delay while the pot cools to the correct temperature. It can't be too moist or too dry, and these shelves are also full. Unglazed bisque can't be used for liquid or food as it is still porous so has limited use. It's interesting that whether you see yourself as a tiny earring or a huge urn in God's scheme of things, the firing takes the same amount of time. The process can't be shortened for smaller objects.

Someone else may be in the pre-glaze phase where sometimes sandpaper is used to smooth any lingering rough patches. Ouch! Then the design and colour are applied by painting or etching and the gloss firing occurs at approximately 1270°C to produce something unique. Finally there are the shelves of skillfully made, finished pieces, gleaming as the light from the window bounces off and displays them for all to see. Which shelf are you on?

A friend has just sent me a stimulating article called *The Tea Cup*, author unknown, which provides a slightly different slant on the pottery process and adds further meaning to my observations:

> *There was a couple who used to go to England to shop in a beautiful antique store. This trip was to celebrate their 25th wedding anniversary. They both liked antiques and pottery, and especially tea cups.*
>
> *Spotting an exceptional cup, they asked, "May we see that? We've never seen a cup quite so beautiful."*
>
> *As the lady handed it to them, suddenly the tea cup spoke, "You don't understand. I have not always been a tea cup. There was a time when I was just a lump of red clay. My master took me and rolled me, pounded and patted me over and over, and I yelled out, 'Don't do that. I don't like it! Let me alone,' but he only smiled, and gently said, 'Not yet!'*
>
> *"Then... WHAM! I was placed on a spinning wheel and suddenly I was spun around and around and around. 'Stop it! I'm getting so dizzy! I'm going to be sick!' I screamed. But the master only nodded and quietly said, 'Not yet.' He spun me and poked and prodded and bent me out of shape to suit himself and then... then he put me in the oven. I never felt such heat. I yelled and knocked and pounded at the door. 'Help! Get me out of here!' I could see him through the opening and I could read his*

SHAPED

lips as he shook his head from side to side, 'Not yet.' When I thought I couldn't bear it another minute, the door opened. He carefully took me out and put me on the shelf, and I began to cool.

"Oh, that felt so good! Ah, this is much better, I thought. But, after I cooled, he picked me up and he brushed and painted me all over. The fumes were horrible. I thought I would gag. 'Oh, please, stop it, stop it!!' I cried. He only shook his head and said, 'Not yet!'

"Then suddenly he put me back in to the oven. Only it was not like the first one. This was twice as hot and I just knew I would suffocate. I begged. I pleaded. I screamed. I cried. I was convinced I would never make it. I was ready to give up. Just then the door opened and he took me out and again placed me on the shelf, where I cooled and waited... and waited... wondering, 'What's he going to do to me next?'

"An hour later he handed me a mirror and said, 'Look at yourself.' And I did. I said, 'That's not me. That couldn't be me. It's beautiful. I'm beautiful!'

"Quietly he spoke: 'I want you to remember back to the beginning,' he said. 'I know it hurt to be rolled and pounded and patted but, had I just left you alone, you'd have dried up. I know it made you dizzy to spin around on the wheel but, if I had stopped, you would have crumbled. I know it hurt, and it was hot and disagreeable in the oven but, if I hadn't put you there, you would have cracked. I know the fumes were bad when I brushed and painted you all over but, if I hadn't done that, you never would have hardened. You would not have had any colour in your life. If I hadn't put you back in that second oven, you wouldn't have survived for long because the hardness would not have held. Now you are *a finished product. Now you are what I had in mind when I first began with you."'*

The moral of this story is: God knows what he is doing with each of us. He is the Potter, and we are his clay. He will mould us and make us, and expose us to just enough pressures - of just the right kinds - so that we may be made into a flawless piece of work to fulfil his good, pleasing and perfect will.

So... when life seems hard, and you are being pounded and patted and pushed almost beyond endurance; when your world seems to be spinning out of control; when you feel like you are in a fiery furnace of trials; when life seems to "stink", try this ... brew a cup of your favourite tea in your nicest tea cup, sit down, and think of this story. Then have a talk with the Potter.

What great advice!

As I've scrolled back over my life I've relived my doubts and disappointments, resentments and ignorance. I often wanted to run away to a deserted island where there were no people and no pain. Jonah tried to run and look where he ended up! Fleeing from the furnace isn't an option because you realise God is right there with you, keeping the temperature just right to achieve the right result.

My scrolling also revealed purpose and peace, blessings, contentment and fulfilment. Taking risks with God is life changing and rewarding. Such an adventure! What an incredible God who loves us as we are but too much to leave us that way. Have you begun your journey with God? It's the best route to find yourself, unravel the past and finally travel to where you're meant to be. If you're bent by life, put yourself in the hands of the Divine Potter.

SHAPED

These lyrics, written by Bill Gaither, sum up my life's journey and you can make this your triumphant story as well.

Something beautiful, something good
All my confusion he understood
All I had to offer him was brokenness and strife
But he made something beautiful of my life.

Postscript

My love/hate relationship with Callan Park/Rozelle Hospital began by being terrified of it as a child to finding it a place of fascination and learning as an adult. For me it's a place of contradictory beauty – warm sandstone on the outside with lawns, gardens and softening river views, wrapped around its cold impersonal heart that was a prison for so many.

The Kirkbride Centre continued to be used for patients until 1994 when the last remaining services were transferred to Broughton Hall on the same site. The NSW Writers Centre and Sydney College of Arts moved into the park in 1996 after restoration was done on the main neo-classic complex. Elsewhere historic buildings are covered in graffiti, have smashed windows or are burnt out. These were the years when the artists took over the asylum! It became a serene and creative venue for writers, painters, photographers, sculptors and potters. In 2008 the remaining patients were moved to Concord Hospital and the complex was placed on the New South Wales State Heritage Register. The government now restricts future uses of the site to health and education purposes.

Visitors can currently use the grounds for a reflective picnic, passive recreation or cycling. You can book yourself in for an historical walking tour or a paranormal tour after dark. Apparently some people think

Callan Park is the most haunted place in Sydney. What are you waiting for?

(See photo insert page B)

The following article appeared in a Sydney newspaper recently.

**Eeriness of Callan Park gives
Ravenswood film crew the creeps**

Kimberley Caines, Inner West Courier Inner City

January 9, 2017

A cast member refused to return to a film set at an abandoned psychiatric hospital in Rozelle as 'spirits whispered in his ears'.

The supernatural horror feature film, *Ravenswood*, was mostly shot in Callan Park, over two weeks last year with 40 crew members.

It follows four US tourists – Sofia (Madeline Marie Dona), Carl (Adam Horner), Belle (Isabel Dickson) and Michael (Shane Savage) – on a vacation to Sydney who decide to go on a ghost tour of Ravenswood.

The movie is due for world-wide release in 2017.

Endorsements

DAWN OF HOPE (BOOK 1) AND KEPT BY LOVE (BOOK 2)

Just finished reading *Dawn of Hope* and loved it! It tugged on the heart strings while shedding light on important life struggles, all the while providing comic relief and a valuable insight into my favourite line of work. A great read. ***AMY***

You write well, with great clarity, your characters are likable and the story pulls the reader along. Your experience in your fields is impressive and I admire the way you've translated all that wisdom into a novella that's insightful and charming at the same time. ***RD***

Having been a Funeral Celebrant and Hospital Chaplain for many years myself, I identified completely with the characters and situations you wrote about. Couldn't put the books down. Who says men don't read fiction? Keep writing! ***DON***

Dawn of Hope was a very entertaining and easy book to read. Thoroughly enjoyed the story. ***MARDI***

Read both *Dawn of Hope* and *Kept by Love* and appreciated the depth of personal conflicts that occurred in the lives of the characters, keeping the reader in anguish. Liked the tension re outcomes and the subtle challenge of the Christian input. The flowing beauty of the wording throughout both books is to be congratulated. The deepest acceptance for me was because I knew you and so much written reflected your life! ***JULIE***

The story of Toni and her struggle with the mental problems in her life touches all of us who recognise the same problems - if not in our own lives, in that of our families and friends. ***CHRIS***

Beautifully written, captivating stories of love and understanding.
ANNE

Loved both your books and really looking forward to your new one. Keep up the good work. **LYN & JOHN**

Dawn of Hope and the sequel *Kept by Love* have a positive message for young people who may have a mental illness. The books explore the reality of having such an illness and the acceptance of needing ongoing medication to stay well and as a result, being able to still have a fulfilling and happy life. The second book shows that despite setbacks, the importance of love, loyalty and forgiveness are paramount in managing challenging situations.

Both books tell a very encouraging story that gives hope to those who struggle with long term mental health issues. **FRAN**

Dawn of Hope — This story, although fiction, is so true to real life. It is an inspiration, humorous, touching and full of faith and hope. I really enjoyed it and couldn't wait for the sequel.

Kept by Love — Funny, sad, full of practical information about wills, funerals, and an insight into mental health. At the same time a beautiful story full of faith and love with a happy ending. **ELIZABETH**

My teenage years were spent caring for my grandmother whose mental health was failing. My once close extended family became divided and distant leaving me with lots of unanswered questions. These novellas helped explain a lot of those lingering questions. **JH**

A very good read. Great learning curve and impactful. First 2 pages had me hooked. Shows a unique understanding of people struggling with life. **CM**

Other books by Kaye

Dawn Of Hope

Book 1

ISBN: 978-0-9875839-0-1

Publisher: arkhousepress.com

From hospital to hope,

from brokenness to wholeness—

could it happen for her?

In Sydney, Australia, in the 21st century, it is still difficult to be different. Despite anti-discrimination and equal opportunity laws, there are social stigmas firmly in place and Toni is again fighting for survival. Will her secret have to remain hidden forever?

Falling in love with her sister's boyfriend is her first obstacle, and coming to terms with her father's death unpacks some surprising revelations.

Working with animals is more rewarding than competing with humans and throwing herself into her job provides humor and light relief in her world of struggle and misunderstanding.

But Toni soon realizes she wants more from life. She wants love, an enduring relationship and a meaningful future. As she explores faith and loss, self-acceptance and purpose, she takes us on a heart-warming journey through sadness and doubt, mirth and elation, to unknown possibilities.

Other books by Kaye

Kept By Love

Book 2

ISBN: 978-0-9923452-6-6

Publisher: arkhousepress.com

As her perfect world begins to crumble, can she find strength to cope with dashed hopes and shattered emotions?

To accept yourself, like what you see, and acknowledge that others like what they see, had been a long process for Toni. For over a year she'd been basking in the warmth of being married to the man of her dreams and working in a new career she loved, but vulnerability and uncertainty were never far from the surface.

She couldn't know that someone unexpected would enter her life, revealing hidden secrets from the past and neither was she prepared for established norms to irrevocably change and be tested.

Being married meant learning to communicate at a deeper level, sharing plans and goals, and she begins to question life and belief. What did she have to contribute? How do you move forward during the tough times?

As we journey with Toni again, we share her laughter and tears as she tries to balance doubt and faith, loss and blessing, sadness and joy. Will she lose herself in the fight to survive or discover what really matters in life?

Callan Park Hospital from Iron Cove
Photo: Phillip Marsh
www.callanpark.com

Archive image Callan Park Gates 1962
Catalogue of State Library NSW

Archive image Callan Park Hospital, opened 1878
Catalogue of State Library NSW

View of Callan Park Hospital showing 'ha ha wall'
Photo: Adam FWC – own work via Commons, 30 December 2014
www.en.wikipedia.org

A

Above: Vandalisation, Rear Ward D, Building 30, Callan Park;
Below: Vandalisation, Rear Ward E, Building 30A, Callan Park
Photos: Garry Burton 10 December 2010
www.garry@gazpixs.com.au

B

Above: Entrance gates Gladesville Hospital
Photo: Sardaka, 15 January 2009 (UTC) - own

Gladesville Hospital
Photo: Curt Flood
Catalogue of State Library NSW

Wards 17 & 18 Gladesville Hospital
Photo: Sardaka
15 January 2009 (UTC) - own

Clockwise from top: The headstone of my grandparents; Still reading and swimming!

www.ingramcontent.com/pod-product-compliance
Lightning Source LLC
Chambersburg PA
CBHW070157100426
42743CB00013B/2941